W9-CKL-762

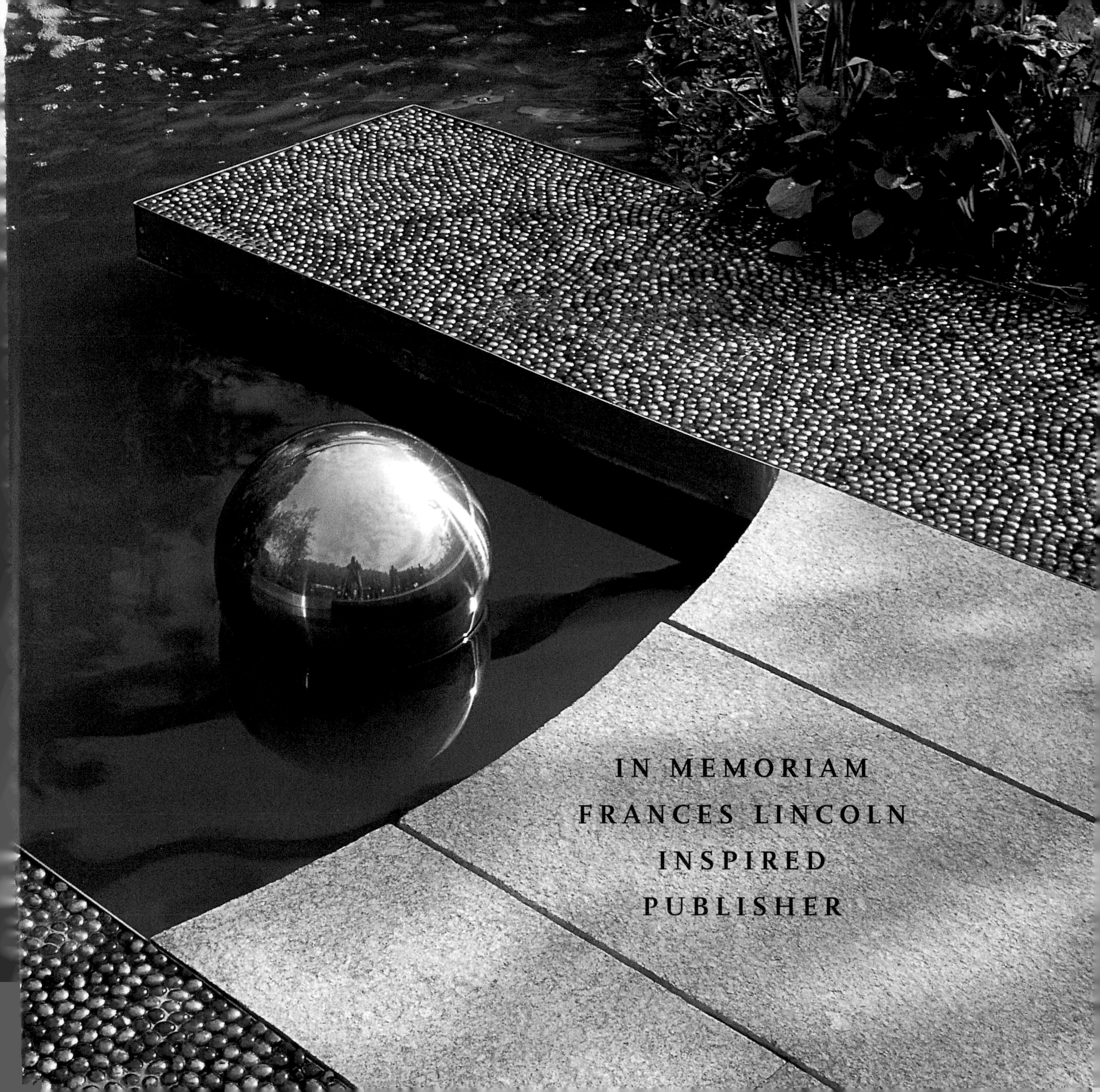

IN MEMORIAM
FRANCES LINCOLN
INSPIRED
PUBLISHER

ROY STRONG

ORNAMENT IN THE SMALL GARDEN

FIREFLY BOOKS

A FIREFLY BOOK

Published by Firefly Books Ltd. 2002

First Printing

National Library of Canada Cataloguing in Publication Data
Strong, Roy, 1935-
Ornament in the small garden
Includes bibliographical references and index.
ISBN 1-55297-561-4 (bound) ISBN 1-55297-560-6 (pbk.)

1. Garden ornaments and furniture. I. Title.
SB473.5.S85 2002 717 C2001-901493-7

U.S. Cataloguing in Publication Data
(Library of Congress Standards)
Strong, Roy.
Ornament for the small garden / Roy Strong. – 1st ed.
144 p. : col. photos. ; cm.
Includes bibliographic references and index.
Summary: A guide and plans to using decorative elements in your garden.
ISBN 1-55297-561-4 (bound) ISBN 1-55297-560-6 (pbk.)
1. Gardens—Design. 2. Landscape gardening. I. Title.
635.9 21 2002 CIP

Published in Canada in 2002 by
Firefly Books Ltd.
3680 Victoria Park Avenue
Willowdale, Ontario M2H 3K1

Published in the United States in 2002 by
Firefly Books (U.S.) Inc.
P.O. Box 1338, Ellicott Station
Buffalo, New York 14205

PAGE 1 Reflective water, a gleaming metallic ball and glittering blue mosaic pebbles contrast with the plain, smooth surface of stone to make a crisp essay in contemporary ornament.

PAGES 2 AND 3 This elegantly decorative open-work fence looks as eye-catching in winter mantled in snow as it will during summer silhouetted against the greens of the hedge.

THIS PAGE In a startling reversal of roles, garden rooms have been made of brilliantly coloured walls rather than green hedges and a living cactus is the central focal point, which can either be encountered through the opening in the foreground or glimpsed through the square aperture cut in the wall opposite.

CONTENTS

DISCOVERING ORNAMENT

I have just come in from walking around The Laskett garden on a chill early February day. Created almost thirty years ago, largely from an open field, and stretching now over some four acres, it can hardly be called a small garden. And yet in a sense it is, for it is made up of a series of small gardens, each one a compartment or a corridor beckoning the visitor to new delights and surprises. The leaves on the trees have long since fallen, leaving only the beauty of the pattern of the branches against the sky and the differing textures of the bark to contemplate. A few berries and fruits, those not taken by the birds, still spangle trees like the *Crataegus crus-galli* which I can see from my writing-room window. And for blossom there are hellebores in plenty along with the earliest spring flowers, snowdrops, crocus, aconites and puschkinias. All of this gives joy, but these incidents would add up to little without the keen delight and satisfaction gained from the garden's geometry and architecture. Dense green yew, clipped into hedges with swags and crenellations or standing as single topiary specimens, is a handsome sight in winter's sunshine. Beech which retains its rich caramel leaves adds a different colour to the palette, as do the myriad greens of thuja and juniper, box and holly. Nor should one forget the splashes of gold afforded by fastigiate golden yew and gilt-edged ilex. It is these seemingly fallow months which provide the yardstick by which to judge the success of a garden. But there is something else which needs to be added to that list: ornament.

Ornament was always in my mind from the moment my wife and I embarked on The Laskett garden in 1973. At that period my point of departure was unashamedly nostalgic, pictures of the great gardens of Renaissance and Baroque Italy with their statues of classical gods and goddesses, stately steps, mysterious grottoes and plashing fountains. To those were added similar pictures, but of the vanished country house gardens of Edwardian England, the world of Miss Jekyll and Sir Edwin Lutyens, gardens articulated by the use of weathered brick and stone, a world of herringbone paths, handsome gate piers, trickling rills, sundials and pergolas. Those were the dreams to which I aspired, ones in which I hoped the inhabitants of Olympus would one day also terminate our garden vistas or flank entrances saluting the visitor and in which a sturdy brick-piered wisteria-hung pergola would lead us onwards.

But, alas, such a garden calls for a substantial chequebook, of a kind I did not have. However, we did what anyone should do in making a garden: got on with the planting, leaving spaces for the ornaments which would come as and when we could afford them. In the meantime I fudged things as best I could, for instance piling up rocks, which I found on site in the middle of what is now the Rose Garden, to form some sort of rudimentary focal point. Today I have replaced that with a handsome stone urn. But it is a point worth making. Ornament need not happen in a day. It can be a cumulative affair built up over the years. That is why I counsel not cementing items down

LEFT This view across the Silver Jubilee Garden to the Rose Garden was taken in the early 1990s. The choice of ornaments, placed to accentuate the formal symmetry and perspective of the garden and to lead the eye on into the distance, reflects a desire at that period to create an atmosphere redolent of Edwardian country house gardens. In less than a decade much of this had been altered or replaced (see page 15).

LEFT Incised on a slate roundel on the ground at the entrance to the main garden are the entwined initials of my wife, Julia Trevelyan Oman, and myself, the date when we started the garden, 1973, and the Latin word 'Circumspice' (Look around). It is an allusion to the famous memorial in St Paul's Cathedral, London, to its architect Sir Christopher Wren: 'If you wish to see his monument, look around.' Ours, therefore, exhorts visitors to look at the garden we made together.

LEFT The Shakespeare Monument was the garden's first important ornament. It is a reproduction, in reconstituted stone, of an urn designed by William Kent now at Longleat House, in Wiltshire. Including the steps and pedestal, it stands about three metres (nearly ten feet) high, and occupies what is perhaps the garden's grandest site – the convergence of its two longest, most spectacular vistas. It was erected and named in 1980 to commemorate being given an award called the Shakespeare Prize, but it was not until over a decade later that that fact was personalized by the addition of the commissioned inset oval plaques showing a portrait of the playwright and the logo of the prize-givers. By then we were experimenting with colour, and the washes of blue and honey yellow were added as part of the scheme that unites the whole garden. The finial on the top was later gilded.

RIGHT The Victoria & Albert Museum Temple, flanked by busts of the Queen and her Consort, is the culmination of a long upward vista from the Shakespeare Monument. That space had remained blank until 1988, a year after I resigned the directorship of the Museum when I was presented with the plaque that now hangs on the back wall of the temple which was constructed to house it. Carved in marble by Simon Verity the plaque depicts my own profile sandwiched between those of the queen and prince. Everyone smiles when they see it. Elements from a catalogue of reconstituted stone architectural ornament were used for the building, while ordinary trellis supports the riot of bloom: *Rosa* 'Paul's Himalayan Musk' and *Rosa* 'Veilchenblau', together with *Clematis* 'Elizabeth' and *Vitis coignetiae*. Later came the garden's signature colours of blue and yellow and the inscription in Greek: 'Memory, Mother of the Muses'.

initially, for you will find that as you acquire better things, you will want to move the earlier ones. Also first sitings are often the wrong ones – as the garden grows or its structure changes, some ornaments suddenly seem ill-placed.

Siting is always crucial. I recall making endless rough groundplans, marking where an ornament should eventually go. What the ornament exactly would be was unclear in my mind but there would definitely be something. For years we had vistas which culminated in a blank space, but I knew that in the end they would be filled, as indeed they have been. But that took thirty years and we are still not wholly complete.

Let me say at once that I have no snobbery about garden ornament. Over the years our garden has taken in everything from reconstituted stone statues, urns and balustrading to antique pieces with fascinating histories, from concrete paviours purchased in the nearest garden centre, to Victorian ironwork and tiles from architectural salvage firms, from found objects, like broken china, to arches and trellis bought off the peg from a catalogue. Old and new are intermingled and the cheap jostles comfortably with the costly. Handled with skill and imagination they all form part of the same composition.

The earliest ornaments to arrive were indeed out of a catalogue; they were reproductions, in reconstituted stone, of originals often found in the gardens of some of the great English country houses. The excitement of the arrival in a van of the first two stone finials and an obelisk, all in pieces which

I had to assemble, is difficult to recapture. They were to be part of my first attempt at a parterre in a yew room just planted. The finials were in the beds and the obelisk formed a terminating exclamation mark. All have long since migrated several times until they have finally come to rest, the finials on pedestals flanking a yew arch and the obelisk set as the culmination of a long vista from the Rose Garden.

This was but a preliminary canter. The first really serious ornament I could afford was again a reproduction, this time a facsimile of an imposing eighteenth-century urn. It was bought in 1980, the year I was given the Shakespeare Prize by a German foundation. I told the donors that the award money would commemorate the event in our garden. That decision prompted us to spread the commemorative concept through the rest of the garden. So what we call the Victoria & Albert Museum Temple, a small classical building, was erected in 1988 to mark the end of my fourteen years as the Museum's director. Later we added an inscription on the pediment, which says, in Greek, 'Memory, Mother of the Muses'. The Muses dwelt in a museum, our lives have been spent in the arts, and the garden in all its aspects was about memory, above all of our own lives and of our friends.

That inscription was a commissioned piece. The journey, therefore, had been made from reproduction to original. The inscription also represented something else pertinent to garden ornament: it can be embroidered upon. That Shakespeare

Monument now sports two added plaques which spell out what it is about. Artists and craftsmen need work and garden pieces need not be costly commissions. Inscriptions are not expensive and give rich resonances to a place. One of my favourites is the roundel of slate at our garden's entrance (see page 7). Another adorns the base of a recumbent stone stag whose antlers have been painted gold: 'a circling row Of goodliest Trees loaden with fairest of Fruit, Blossoms and Fruit at once of golden hue Appeerd, with gay enameld colours mixt:'. Encircled with a ceramic garland of fruit and flowers, these lines, from the description of the Garden of Eden in John Milton's epic poem *Paradise Lost,* speak of blossom and golden fruit and are perfect for the orchard over which the beast presides.

Over the years we have moved on from that tribute to the classical tradition. Colour has been one of our greatest discoveries. When we started gardening the vogue was for everything to be distressed. The phoney effect of moss- and lichen-decked ornament, crumbling seemingly from the hand of centuries, was achieved by painting a raw item with sour milk or yogurt. It took some time to discover that this passion for antiquing was a late-nineteenth-century phenomenon. In the past, garden ornament was often in bright and garish colours with an abundance of paint finishes from gilding to marbling. Those lead statues of shepherds and shepherdesses which graced the formal gardens of early Georgian England, for example, were once polychrome, and often placed not on pedestals but dotted around to give the illusion that they were real, thus transforming the garden into Arcady.

Some of our earliest experiments were with gold, first gold paint and later gold leaf. Paint, sad to say, is no substitute for leaf. But, I must add, it matters little in the garden how crude the gilding is. A reconstituted stone ball on top of a pillar was gilded. It stands at the end of a long vista and sparkles wondrously when it catches the sun. In winter the effect is breathtaking. Metal plant supports that had finials like roses were painted gold, their stems blue. And that led eventually to our even bolder decision to give the whole garden a colour identity, what we now refer to as the garden's livery colours of blue and yellow. The blue was inspired by a visit to Russia, glimpsed on buildings in St Petersburg under snow. The yellow, which tends to ochre, came from a visit to country houses in Bohemia and Moravia. It is a colour that one sees used everywhere in Europe on buildings in the rococo period of the mid-eighteenth century.

Using ordinary household emulsion paint, we started to trick out various parts of the architecture and ornaments in the garden with the yellow. The inset panels on all the pedestals were painted. The effect was quite extraordinary, for suddenly it linked old and new, genuine and phoney, right through the garden. The blue was used rather less than the yellow but looked particularly good on anything metallic, although the Shakespeare Monument had the bowl of its urn picked out with the colour – a decision which called for some nerve – and the stone column at the other end of the vista was painted to echo it. In the form of wood stain, the blue colour was applied to all the trellis and treillage in the garden, tunnels and single arches as well as pergolas and screening. And, finally, and bravest of all, the house and its conservatory were painted in the same livery, thus drawing the entire ensemble into one colour scheme.

All of that happened in the early 1990s. By then I was irritated by books on colour in the garden which never included ornament although it gives colour for all twelve months of the year. We were also aware that garden design was taking one of its periodic lurches forward. Somehow the exultation by the Arts and Crafts movement of natural materials and weathering seemed more and more an anomaly as we moved into the twenty-first century. Our leap was not only one of colour but also of pattern. We decided to have the pleached lime avenue

OPPOSITE AND LEFT The pleached lime avenue was planted in 1981 and called Elizabeth Tudor after my wife and I had collaborated on a little book about that queen in 1971. It stretches some fifty metres (sixty yards) from a reconstituted stone pillar topped by a gilded ball to the Shakespeare Monument.

It is shown (opposite) in the early 1990s with its interior line of fastigiate Irish yews flanking a grass path, and (left) in 1998 after the decision was taken to abolish the turf in favour of paving. The path was designed by my wife, using readily available tinted concrete paviours that are kept pristine by being thoroughly cleaned each year. A low yew hedge, through which standard hollies are being trained, was planted each side of the walk to link the Irish yew pillars. The stone pillar and pedestal are picked out in the garden's livery colours of blue and ochre yellow, and incised slate plaques, inset with the crown and initials of the two queens, Elizabeth I and II, adorn the base of the pedestal.

We laid out the Howdah Court at the close of the 1990s, to a design by my wife. It began with turf that had been excavated for making paths elsewhere being piled up to form a mount or, as we call it, the 'elephant', seen on the left and now covered in creepers. This is straddled by the fantastic howdah made from an assortment of salvaged ornamental ironwork that has been painted a vivid blue. Below the howdah's platform the carved stone crown seems to hover above a reconstituted stone bench. Water spills from what were the caps of two old gate piers, again from a salvage yard. Iron balusters from a builder's materials emporium make pretty tree guards and fencing, and the wooden arches come from a supplier's catalogue. In spring, the yellow and blue theme of the garden is taken into the planting with a dazzling display of brilliant yellow 'Golden Apeldoorn' tulips.

paved and my wife designed a spectacular path using materials of our own time: different-coloured concrete slabs. These were either laid whole or cut in half straight across or diagonally. The result is a walk some fifty metres (sixty yards) long like a Renaissance palace floor (see previous pages). And, contrary to usual practice, we did not intend this to become discoloured and covered with plants. Each spring a pressure water cleaner scrubs its surface bright as new. Since then we have moved on to other paths, this time of old Victorian tiles and industrial brick, but in each the emphasis is on geometric pattern which enlivens the surface and is meant to be seen and admired all through the year.

Our most adventurous foray in terms of ornament is in a new garden at the front of the house. The ground has patterned paving using a mixture of Victorian tiles and concrete paviours. Low fountains have been made out of the caps of two gate piers spotted in a salvage yard, drilled to allow water to bubble up through a rose at the top and slither down the sides into square bowls. A knot garden of clipped heather with sentinels of juniper has been infilled not only with the usual gravel but also, more excitingly, with cullet – offcuts of coloured glass discarded in the blowing process – in the yellow and blue livery colours. Raised beds have been made by upending large concrete paviours and the new beds have been edged with Victorian roofing tiles. Inexpensive off-the-shelf staircase turnings have been set into metal frames to form fences and frame trees. The star piece, however, is what we call the mount, a structure which stands bestride a rectangular mound made of turves. This assemblage of two Victorian spiral staircases, pretty perforated radiator panels and odd fluted iron pillars, all from an architectural salvage yard, is held together by common scaffolding poles. The Howdah Court, as we have named this part of the garden, shows that gardening never stops still, for it has a fantasy and an originality of a kind wholly different from where we started three decades ago. What triggered this mad explosion was a single found object, a large old metal-framed window which my wife spotted in a salvage yard. Now painted blue and standing in one of the raised beds, it provided the starting point for a garden which belongs unequivocally to the present time, to the beginning of the twenty-first century.

RIGHT One of a number of delightful metal plant supports which we purchased in Holland, brought home and personalized by painting the stems blue and applying gold paint to the rose.

OPPOSITE The Silver Jubilee and Rose Gardens changed dramatically during the late 1990s: compare the photograph on page 6 with this one taken in the year 2000. The two central ornaments, an antique sundial and urn, remain the same, but classical urns have replaced the Thai planters in the Silver Jubilee Garden and the statues of the two boy warriors have vanished from the Rose Garden. The clipped yew balls have been axed from the entrance and the four amelanchier trees, one of which died, have been replaced by beech trained as standards.

Two obelisks topped with gilded balls have finally come to rest, after many migrations, flanking a newly erected triumphal arch. That was precipitated by a garden tragedy when the fully grown yew hedge behind it was reduced, through a misunderstanding, to waist height. Something spectacular was needed to deflect the eye from the disaster and hence the arch.

Moveable ornament comes at The Laskett in many forms. An astonishing range of plant containers is always on the move from one place to another. The most striking configuration is just outside the back door into the garden, where a collection of pots is rearranged periodically on a whole forest of different supports from piles of bricks to chimney pots and slabs of stone. This tableau is the first thing that we see on going into the garden. It is called the Treasury, for each season of the year displays some plant treasure to advantage.

On the terrace outside the conservatory is a reconstituted stone table on which sits a handsome pot filled with house leeks which cascade over its sides. That is supported by a display of interesting stones dug up in the garden arranged like a still life, an effect similar to another in the orchard. There a stone trough has been filled with all the broken blue and white china we have unearthed here over the years. It is our garden museum, our display of historic shards. Nor should I forget items like the glistening reflective witch ball which is suspended beneath a ceiling of arching branches, or the odd ceramic ball, of a kind readily obtainable at garden centres, which my wife places as accents in her naturalistic glades.

This plethora of things is, of course, integral to the design of the garden. But how cold that single fact is. True ornament is so much more. In our case it expresses the spirit of The Laskett. It gives the space an identity in a way no plant ever could. It evokes mood and memory. Ornament can mourn and celebrate. It can also be witty. One of my favourites is a monument to a cat, the Reverend Wenceslas Muff. In a small sheltered enclosure there is a pedestal topped with a golden ball. On the side there is a bas-relief of his head wearing clerical bands and inscribed on the panels are his dates and the words 'Loving' and 'Brave', which he was. I never pass this tribute to a much-loved creature without a tear and a smile. It is not far away from perhaps our grandest ornament, a triumphal arch (erected to conceal the unbidden cutting down of a hedge) which bears a message which speaks from the heart: 'Conditor Horti Felicitatis Auctor' (They who plant a garden, plant happiness).

How dull The Laskett garden would be without its ornaments, each one scrimped and saved for, each one enshrining a thought, a memory and, at the same time, integral to its sense of style and balance. Through every season these things greet me like so many old friends, milestones in a lifetime. Cumulatively they tell me that just one ornament chosen with passion and placed with vision bestows on the tiniest space an aura unattainable by any other means. Ornament is indeed the soul of the garden.

CONDITOR·HORTI·FELICITATIS·AVCTOR

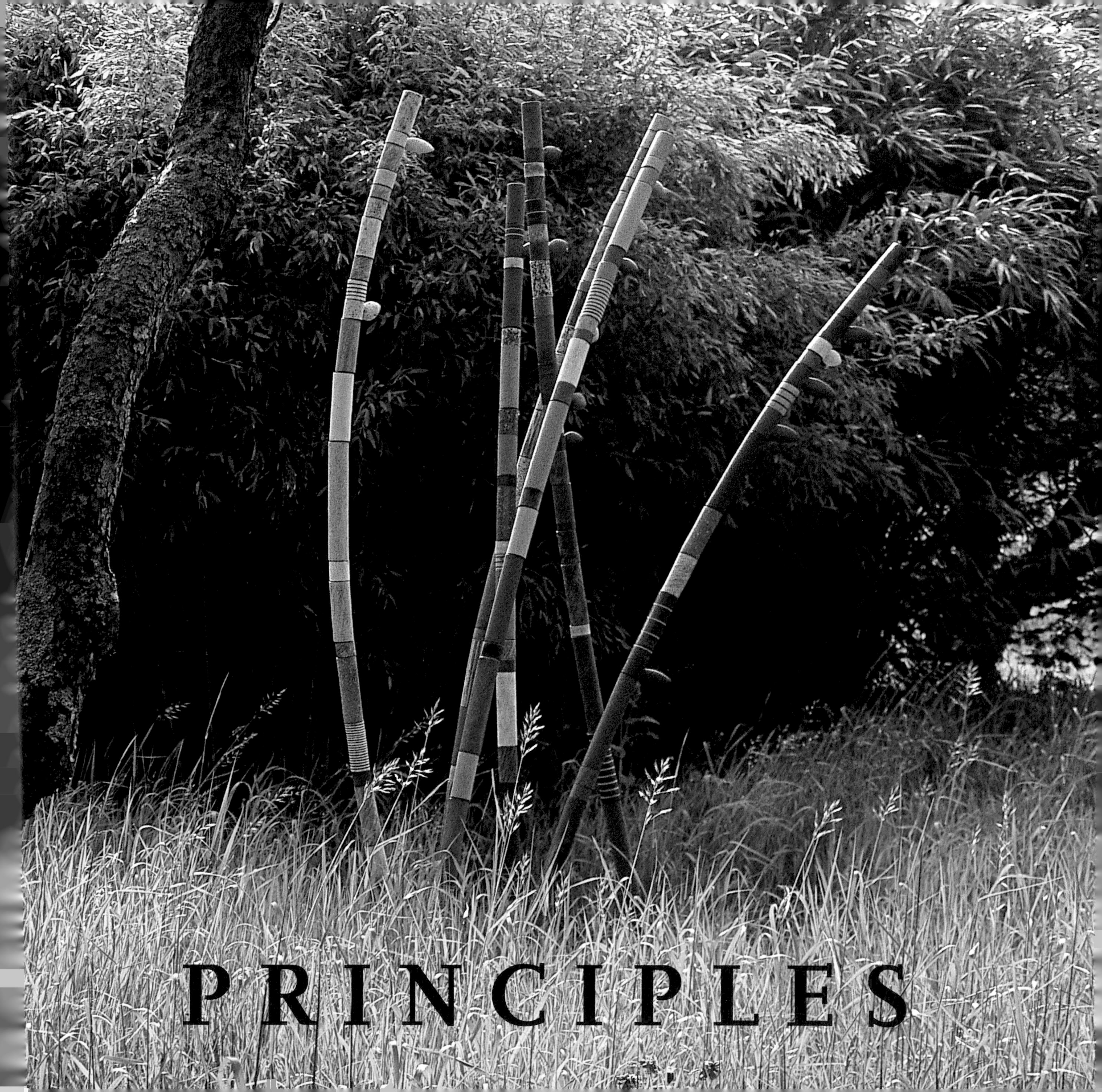

PRINCIPLES

An evergreen clipped into a prehistoric monster towers above the roof of the house giving this garden a startling and quite unexpected aura of fantasy and wit. The owner, one feels, must have a good sense of humour. Topiary sculpture is living ornament.

For many people cultivating a small space, the idea of using ornament can be intimidating. All too often it is associated with an aristocratic past that seems to have little relevance to the way we garden in the egalitarian present. The main reason I have not included a section on the history of ornament is that such an inheritance can be off-putting. Illustrations of the giant Renaissance river gods at the Villa Lante, in Italy, or avenues of statues at Louis XIV's garden at Versailles, or the elaborate eighteenth-century grotto at Stourhead, in Wiltshire, could lead today's gardeners to conclude that ornament is not for them.

Substantial pieces of natural rock disposed as abstract sculpture within a glade of silver birch trees provoke a dialogue about where the world of nature ends and that of art begins. The bold vertical acts as a powerful focal point and a strong textural contrast to the fluttering foliage.

A massive scarecrow, which both amuses and threatens, arises like some apparition, piercing the horizon and towering above the flanking fruit trees. A more moveable ornament, a cut-out metal duck, perches at the water's edge. Both bestow inspired zaniness on what is otherwise a conventional country orchard and pond.

A classically garbed stone nymph gazes at her own reflection in a pool. As well as adding a bold vertical counterpoint to the free-flowing foliage, her elegant presence betrays a nostalgia for times gone by. By placing the figure at ground level she is also figuratively taken off a pedestal and, amid planting at the water's edge, a mood of calm and pensiveness is evoked.

But such a conclusion would be wrong, for effective ornament can be as simple as a single, well-placed ceramic pot, the witty embellishment of a potting shed or a scattering of coloured stones around the foot of a tree, and the principles that govern their use are eternals, as applicable in the smallest of spaces as in the vast acres of a country house garden.

The first principle of ornament is that it should bestow a style and identity on a garden. It is like an apt quotation pinpointing exactly what your garden means to you and what you wish it to tell the visitor.

Contemporary movements in sculpture using found objects and all kinds of natural phenomena have totally released the garden maker from the confines of the past and more or less anything goes in today's world as long as it expresses your identity and contributes to your vision. Ornament can say more about your own predilections than almost anything else in the garden whether it takes the form of a major statement, such as a gothic gazebo, or a series of small incidents, such as a collection of old watering cans, a secluded wooden seat or a row of brightly painted plant supports. Nostalgic or quirky, romantic or ruthlessly minimalist, ornament can amuse, charm or challenge. But like the style of interior decoration of your house, all these elements will speak volumes to the visitor about your taste and ideas.

The range of reactions which it is possible to trigger in the onlooker is limitless. By means of allusion, an ornament and its setting can, in addition, set in train a host of references to the world of art, literature, politics, private life or, indeed, to other gardens. For example, if you choose a classical urn or statue as a major feature, you place your garden within a line of descent which goes back to the Renaissance, when excavated Roman statuary was first used to adorn the garden, but you also send out signals about nostalgia and intimations of grandeur. A line of jagged rocks erupting across a lawn, on the other hand, reveals an uncompromisingly contemporary outlook. Bird tables and nesting boxes register a commitment to sustaining birdlife and a handsome hand-thrown pot indicates a passion for traditional crafts. An arrangement of pebbles or stones can denote a feeling for natural materials or an interest in geology but, like many ornaments, may also privately evoke memories of where they were acquired. More subliminally, some ornaments enshrine stability and permanence amid wispy, ephemeral planting, while others may come and go, emphasizing the flux of the seasons.

The immediate setting for an ornament leads on from questions of style to a consideration of something much deeper: mood. Exactly the same ornament can completely change mood according to its context. A pair of clean-cut, classical urns flanking an entrance will reveal a taste for tradition, but also suggest symmetry and good order. The same urns, covered in lichen and moss and dripping with fronds of ivy, glimpsed from afar and arranged asymmetrically in a tangled glade, will call to mind very different thoughts, ones of mystery and melancholy.

Sensitivity to context is crucial. The choice of location in terms of planting and light conditions, as well as how the ornament is first encountered, can make all the difference to how it is perceived. The element of surprise is always welcome, whether it involves turning a corner and suddenly coming upon a hitherto concealed ornament, or discovering an unexpected contrast between ornament and setting, such as that between the clean-cut lines of a formal obelisk in a wild flower meadow.

Establishing identity while evoking allusion and conjuring an atmosphere are the primary principles of ornament. But ornament can also have a more practical role, as an essential part of the design of your garden, one which presents you with a delectable bag of optical tricks. I still have the groundplan sketches, only approximate and by no means to scale, which I made of The Laskett in 1973. In these I did what I suggest anyone embarking on a garden should do: I divided up the area into the spaces I had in mind, emphasizing sight lines and focal points. I took into consideration any changes of level that called for a step or more, those things that I wished to obliterate from sight and those that I wanted to include, such as glimpses of the

FAR LEFT A swathe of lawn leading to an informal boundary planting of trees and shrubs with a panorama of landscape beyond is given a heady romanticism by the addition of a rose-covered temple. The mood is of a *recherche du temps perdu*.

LEFT A mirror glass obelisk and a serpentine line of stainless-steel posts provide a striking counterpoint to the engulfing ox-eye daisies and trees in full leaf beyond. While the forms of the ornaments are totally traditional, the materials with which they are made are strictly of our own time. Hard-edged and permanent in themselves, the effect they make when placed, seemingly haphazardly, in a field of flowers is romantic, with the bonus of tantalizing reflections.

landscape beyond. On to the sketches I marked the places where, one day, ornaments should be placed. As I said in my introduction, I did not always know what the ornament would be, but I knew where and why it was needed.

It is true that I was working with a blank canvas, while the majority of people who are thinking about ornament will be faced with an existing garden, usually made by someone else. But the guidelines for exploiting the potential of ornament apply as much to those wanting to alter a garden as to those who are starting with an empty expanse.

It almost goes without saying that any ornament immediately draws the eye. Occasionally a natural feature, such as a tree or a piece of topiary, can fulfil the same function but when it does this, it is precisely because it is acting as a permanent ornament. The fact that vision can be controlled by ornament – hastened, slowed down or stopped, somewhat like responding to traffic signals – is worth using to advantage. Pairs of almost anything, piers with urns atop them, for instance, warn visitors that they are about to move out of one area into another, whether or not through a formal entrance. Smaller or more detailed ornaments, particularly those meant to be seen close-to, such as an inscribed stone, may cause the viewer to stop in contemplation for a moment; while other ornaments, seen first at a distance, lure the eye and foot to travel from one spot to another, aided by another weapon in the armoury of the garden designer – the path.

Sight lines – the lines along which the eye is drawn – can take two forms. They can literally be direct, taking you to the ornament by means of a straight path flanked by clipped hedges, an avenue of pleached trees or a pair of borders. Alternatively the treatment can be more relaxed, with a path, flanked by asymmetric planting, that meanders towards the ornament, affording occasional glimpses of it from afar to lead the viewer on. The aim of both is the same: to control the way

RIGHT A simple obelisk, placed at the end of a major vista, performs a multiplicity of roles. It immediately bestows a sense of place, its classical form transforming a pretty glade into a vision of Arcady. A strong, vertical accent, it draws the eye, and in so doing visually lengthens the mown grass path, while its sharp outline forms a striking contrast to the frothy foliage that surrounds it. Such an effect is simplicity itself, calling only for an ornament that is readily available in reconstituted stone.

RIGHT Here the eye is taken for a walk from the terrace next to the house across a stretch of greensward into the woodland beyond by means of angular pieces of stone sunk into the turf. Seemingly simple, it is in fact a highly sophisticated piece of professional garden making. In practical terms it would call for careful cutting of the grass.

LEFT Arranged like a boldly framed still life painting, this small Japanese-inspired garden owes much of its success to its hard surfaces which ascend in steps, giving an illusion of more depth than is the reality, and also to the skilful disposition of stones and ceramic containers nestling beneath the arching greenery.

RIGHT A rhythmic statue which doubles as a seat is silhouetted against a yew hedge and positioned to make the most of the slanting rays of the winter sun. Framed by a rose arch, which helps to draw the eye, it makes a bold termination to a walk.

the eye perceives the ornament and how visitors wend their way towards it.

When placing your major focal points, it may be helpful to relate the control of sight lines in a garden to an old-fashioned picture-frame stage set. This used diminishing side wings to suggest receding space, with a backcloth painted with the lines of perspective meeting at a single vanishing point to suggest infinity. Exploiting the effect of colour tonality, using dark and bright colours in the foreground and pale ones in the distance, added to the sense of vista. If you think of your garden as a series of toy theatre peepshows you will not go far wrong in attaining a classical disposition of ornament within this space; whether placed dead centre, in the distance or in the foreground will depend on the stage picture you are seeking to evoke.

The fact that historic theatre design worked from the premise that things appear smaller in the distance is a reminder that clever placing can make a small ornament seem far larger. This can be achieved by placing the object afar, ideally at the close of an upward slope, and narrowing the lines of planting the nearer they get to the object.

The dramatic pictorial effect can be further enhanced by framing the ornament so that it is seen, for example, through a rose arch or a gate, or at the end of a pergola or an avenue of trees or clipped hedges. Framing also bestows greater prominence and significance on an ornament and will hold a group of smaller, more disparate pieces together, giving them cohesion.

So far I have concentrated on the placing of major ornaments within a small space but what of minor ones? The drive towards the one major piece may include incidents along the way which momentarily arrest the eye, such as a decorative mosaic set within the paving of a path. A row of decorative plant supports can give structure in a border, a pretty seat painted a striking colour will set off a clipped hedge, and a nesting box provide punctuation of colour and shape in the greenery of a treescape. Smaller decorative details, such as tile edging for a path or finials on fencing posts, also add variety to the forms, colours and textures in the garden.

Some of the most versatile minor ornaments are those that are moveable. The range is limitless, from simple *trompe l'oeil* cut-outs to tablescapes – assemblages of favourite objects – all

of which can be rearranged to compose a different picture, according to your inclination.

It is, of course, possible to base a whole garden on small incidents, but it is usually only successful if these are strongly linked through a theme, style or colour. A plethora of small ornaments, unless very carefully orchestrated and controlled, can quickly fragment into an accumulation of meaningless clutter, giving confusing and contradictory signals. My advice would be always to concentrate on the major statement.

If I had to cite the single most glaring fault of those who deploy ornament in small gardens it would be equating a small garden with small ornament. In a small garden where there is space for only one major statement, that main ornament must be of a scale to be noticed, to bestow instant identity and also hold a scheme together through the seasons. Even in a small garden it calls for something at least a metre (over three feet) high, preferably more. It is often forgotten that ornaments are not only to be looked down upon and looked directly at but also to be looked up to. The skyline is a crucial part of any garden's composition. It is made up chiefly of the tree and shrub line, but

it can also include tall ornaments like a weather-vane on a summerhouse or a dovecote. Even a small unimportant statue becomes a commanding presence if placed atop a column. Raising the height of an ornament is one means of making a major focal point with very limited resources.

Because placing is so important, do experiment with it. It is worth making some kind of rough cut-out of the shape and placing it in different positions to get an idea of its effect. At least push a bamboo into the ground to consider the required height. There is no substitute for the actual thing, but such exercises provoke thought about the visual impact of the ornament on the garden. I find that ornaments do not always end up where they were first envisioned, so think carefully before you fix something permanently.

Never forget that ornaments differ from the other elements in a garden's composition in that they do not change with the seasons. Most are *in situ* for all twelve months of the year, and you will be looking at them in winter, spring, summer and

LEFT Practical buildings like sheds and garages can be garden eyesores. Here a utilitarian building has been transformed into a delightful pavilion by the brilliant solution of painting it and decorating it with an array of containers and tools, and adding modest paving and treillage screens to form two small terraces from which to view the garden.

RIGHT What would otherwise be a patchy, dull, blank wall has been enlivened by a bold terracotta colour wash as well as by a planting of flowering climbers. But the eye has already been deflected from the deficiencies of the wall, firstly by a sundial arising from the middle of a tiny herb garden and secondly by the attractive gothic seat painted a pretty shade of blue.

autumn; under snow, covered in frost, lashed by rain and scorched by sun; and when the garden is at its most floriferous as well as when the branches of the trees and shrubs are bare.

The movement of the sun and quality of light must also be considered when siting ornaments. The way that arbours, seats and summerhouses face depends on whether they are to catch the sun or to provide shade. Three-dimensional ornaments like statues should never be situated flat against a hedge or wall but always placed at least half a metre (about eighteen inches) away in order that their plastic qualities are fully realized, and only ornaments with an exceptionally bold silhouette will make any impact if they are placed out of the reach of the sun. Do remember that shadows add greatly to the drama of ornament. Free-standing treillage, for example, will cast intriguing patterns on to the ground. Planting can also be used to manipulate lighting effects, softening an ornament with dappled shade, or, if placed at the end of a pergola, transforming the terminating feature into a striking silhouette when seen against the light.

One of the important supporting roles that ornament can play is to detract from or dress up less attractive features. If you position a colourful, comfortable bench at the end of a path, for example, the eye will be drawn straight to it, cheerfully sliding by any number of deficiencies in a flower border along the way. Or, with an arresting object placed at the garden's boundary, you can often deflect the eye from travelling beyond it to something awful over which you have no control.

In other cases dull but utilitarian items that are necessary within the garden may themselves be disguised and turned into ornamental features. A brutal manhole cover can vanish beneath a planter to be moved only when access to the manhole is required. A blank garage wall is transformed by the application of pretty treillage with climbers, and a dilapidated shed becomes a delightful folly when dressed over with gingerbread fretwork and colour. Never hesitate to be inventive.

All these considerations need to be taken into account at the planning stage, before you start to consider buying ornaments. Once you have given some thought to style and allusion, and settled on the purpose and function of any ornaments, you still have a crucial question to answer, and that is how much can you afford? My advice is always to bear in mind the fact that ornament is practically the only thing in a garden which has an instantaneous effect. So do not stint.

As a starting point, a visit to a good garden centre can be a tremendous help in deciding which direction you will go, and it will also give you an indication on price range. Looking at ornaments in a garden centre is a useful learning experience that helps you to think in terms of scale and placing in your own garden, as well as allowing you to check the suitability of this or that item to the architecture of the house. I would add a stroll through a large builder's yard: there you will find paviours, bricks, varieties of gravel and stone chipping, roof tiles, chimney pots, ranges of ready-cut timber and mouldings, in short a cornucopia of materials which can be pressed into service for garden features from arbours to summerhouses, from temples to pergolas, from paths to steps. I have seen curved roof ridge tiles reversed and sunk into the ground to create a stunning rill, and it is amazing what can be constructed by using drainage pipes as inexpensive columns. The builder's yard is in its way like a painter's palette.

For the ecologically minded the exploration of rubbish tips and skips for pieces that can be recycled as garden ornament is another possibility, and architectural salvage yards can be inspirational. In such repositories you will find weathered brick and stone, odd finials, old garden ornaments, assorted sections of decorative iron railing, a multitude of columns and capitals, window frames of all sizes and shapes, decorative radiator panels, door embrasures, a myriad pieces piled pell-mell in a riot of confusion. Often your eye will alight upon the one thing that will set your garden apart or spot pieces which can either be assembled to make something unique or mingled with the materials of today to give them that extra edge and richness. Items salvaged from demolished buildings offer a fascinating voyage of discovery and invention for the garden maker.

Sales of garden ornaments are now regular events. Star lots may go for many thousands of pounds, but the great majority are run-of-the-mill modern Italian statues in the Baroque manner or architectural fragments like finials, balls, coats of arms,

A spiral of jagged flints unfurls from a metal spring that holds aloft a larger flint. Designed by Ivan Hicks from found elements, this simple but effective device – the stones catch the light and, when wet, change colour – transforms the whole secluded corner into an ornament in its own right, as well as making a setting for the architectural fragment that has become an abstract sculpture. The jagged primeval quality of this craggy whirlpool is cleverly provided with a foil of the soft 'Johnson's Blue' geraniums and *Alchemilla mollis* that surrounds it.

FAR LEFT An inspired, idiosyncratic addition of blue bottles to a tree captures the eye at sky level, a reminder that ornament also has a role to play as aerial decoration.

LEFT Atop a support, a bird house in the form of a miniature church in the neo-classical style complete with a steeple acts as an elegant, if whimsical, punctuation mark in a garden's composition, drawing the eye upwards.

RIGHT Ruins as symbols of mortality and the decay of things have been part of the garden repertory for centuries. Here the theme is captured in miniature with the moss-encrusted bowl of an antique urn lying amid the first flush of snowdrops.

FAR RIGHT Attracting the eye downwards in delight, a pretty incident in a garden stroll is formed by coloured stones scattered like jewels at the foot of a tree.

capitals and odd pieces of carving. The sales usually include a section with nineteenth-century ironwork, in the main a vast array of seats and benches of every kind but also grander pieces like fountains and aviaries, as well as many urns, planters, troughs, busts and pedestals in every style, shape and size. Anything which could conceivably find a buyer is included. The catalogues offer price estimates but these are almost invariably wrong (in most cases overestimates). Unless you are familiar with the workings of auctions, get someone experienced to bid for you, giving that person a ceiling beyond which not to go. Remember that if your bid is successful you may have to add tax and a buyer's premium to the saleroom price plus the cost of transporting the piece. Don't be deterred by all of this: with a keen eye, bargains are to be had. There are also firms which specialize in antique garden ornament, but what they sell is not cheap. If you can run to that price range they are worth visiting, and it is often possible to see what is in stock on the internet.

Antique pieces and items bought from architectural salvage yards can be expensive to move and labour-intensive to erect. You will need help with the unloading and transfer of any substantial items. They may arrive in sections and, although the average gardener might be able to cope with setting up a sundial in three pieces, when it comes to balustrading or a temple you will almost certainly need the services of a professional builder. Inevitably anything large or heavy will be a nightmare to move once sited, so make absolutely certain about its placing. In the case of antique pieces do remember that the theft of garden statuary has reached almost epic proportions. The larger the piece and the more inaccessibly it is sited, the less likely it is to vanish on the back of a lorry overnight.

Long-term maintenance is another factor to consider. You can leave reconstituted stone out in all weathers to accumulate moss and lichen. However, that is not the case with marble or softer stone. These and any good antique pieces need to be bagged for the winter to protect them from the effects of frost. Water penetrating stone or marble and freezing can result in the damage or complete destruction of an ornament. Stone is also subject to atmospheric pollution. Even in the country, a pristine piece can turn literally soot black within a few years. To combat this I have found a high-pressure water cleaner an

invaluable piece of garden equipment, but it must be used with caution. The strong jet blasts off the black sooty deposits but should not be used on any valuable antique piece without seeking advice from a stone conservator. Such radical treatment could do damage and erode detail in the carving.

Do not despise catalogues of mass-manufactured ornament in reconstituted stone, iron and wood. The reconstituted stone catalogues contain ornaments for instant use such as sundials, obelisks and planters as well as a repertory of architectural parts: columns of varying heights, thicknesses and styles, screening and balustrading, and segments from which to construct arches, niches, pergolas and fountains, for example, so that you can put together your own custom-designed water feature, garden house or gazebo. The reconstituted stone supplier will often work with your builder, providing him with an exact specification for the foundations as well as supplying drawings and directions for construction. Although the cost of erection can easily exceed what you have paid for the item, the comfort is that such a substantial outlay bestows instant distinction on a garden.

Firms which specialize in ironwork or simulations of ironwork also produce a huge range of items, particularly reproductions from that golden age of the craft, the Victorian era. Such collections will generally include decorative railings and panels which could act as screening, gates, seats, tables, arches, pergola sections and arbours. Lead ornaments are still produced but more often than not fibreglass is simulated to look like lead. The effect is remarkably convincing and used mainly for reproductions of historic urns and tanks as planters. (Fibreglass is also used to simulate wood in, for instance, highly deceptive facsimiles of Versailles tubs.) Faux is less likely to be stolen than genuine lead, and does not need repainting every few years, unlike ironwork, which rusts if not well maintained.

There is also wood. Of all the materials used in the garden, wood needs the greatest discrimination. It has a finite life and whatever you erect is destined to disintegrate, so be vigilant that any timber is properly seasoned, and preferably comes with a twenty-five-year guarantee. However, its astonishing versatility and low cost does make it ideally suited to the garden, particularly for starter ornaments. Almost anything ornamental

RIGHT A single ornament, here a delightful polychrome gazebo made of painted and decorated wood, gives this garden all it needs. Anything else would merely detract from the composition. The angular lines of the gazebo make a strong counterpoint to the winding path that leads to it, to the froth of flower-decked planting in front of it, and to the tapestry of tree foliage behind it.

FAR RIGHT Poised at the centre of a decoratively planted path that runs between two borders, a modest but handsome hand-thrown terracotta pot holds this extremely effective garden composition together. Simplicity itself, the substantial solidity of the container offsets the wispy, shimmering nature of the grasses planted on either side.

can be run up from timber and it lends itself to a variety of finishes from attractive natural weathering through staining to painting in a solid colour. Wood can be a major vehicle for introducing dramatic colour to the garden picture.

The quality of wood products can vary more than those of stone and metal, both in terms of the timber used and the standard of workmanship. Wooden garden arches and latticework trellis remain classics, but on the whole it is a poor investment when used for any major garden structure. A summerhouse properly built of brick and stone will last a lifetime and far beyond. A poorly made, inexpensive timber one may begin to decay within a decade. Everything made of wood needs attention and, when used to support plants, there is the added complication of unravelling the plant while the support is repaired or replaced. None the less wood has a symbiosis with the garden which makes it easy to place in a composition.

When considering the huge range of potential for garden ornament it is, of course, important to remember that you can mix the media, so take your time before buying. Firms that sell garden ornaments usually have show gardens where their products are on display, or they may take a stand at major flower shows. It is well worth acquiring the catalogues and then visiting the displays to examine the range and quality of the products at first hand.

A classical rotunda built as the termination of an avenue of clipped mophead trees recorded in summer, autumn and snow-clad winter brings home the centrality of ornament to the year-round garden picture. The temple and shapes of the clipped topiary trees remain unchanged through the seasons, providing a strong identity to an essentially Arcadian scene. It is not only the world of nature which changes around it but also the quality of light. The approach by way of the avenue gives a formal edge to a composition which would be equally strong if they were absent but whose resonances would be more sylvan.

In looking at all these hard-surface ornaments, do not forget the role of living ones. Topiary occupies a unique role in the garden for it belongs equally to the world of plants and to that of ornament. Clipped and trained evergreens can be transformed into walls, arches, pilasters, obelisks, columns, even sculpture. Anyone who wishes to understand the role of ornament should also have an understanding and knowledge of the art of topiary.

Finally, do consider the pleasure that can be derived from commissioning a piece from an artist or craftsman. It need not be expensive. Inscriptions are a modest instance of this and they add greatly to a garden's sense of intellectual depth and sense of personality. To commission a fountain or other form of water feature could be costly but would certainly add a unique distinction. But here one touches upon a problem which I regard as central to the understanding of ornament. Ornament is ornament. It makes no attempt to usurp the world of nature and turn the garden into a sculpture park. My own firm view is that a garden is not an art gallery and that garden sculpture in the past was unashamedly decorative, even if invested with meaning. The garden can easily be hijacked by artists, whose

creations refuse to be one mute element in a picture in which trees, shrubs and flowers, together with other artefacts, all have their part to play. When choosing your artist or craftsman, make certain they understand that their contribution is only one part, albeit a significant one, of the overall scene.

I end with a note on planting because all too often the use of ornament in all its various guises can result in the small garden becoming a concrete jungle, a deadening accumulation of hard surfaces with trophies of ailing plants in containers. At its best ornament is something far different. Ideally it should be a perfect marriage with the world of tamed nature that is the garden. This is what was achieved through the centuries in the great gardens we still visit with awe and wonder today. That equilibrium calls for constant vigilance because trees and shrubs grow and the composition constantly changes through the years. What seemed at the outset a bold hard-surface statement can within a few years shrink to insignificance engulfed in foliage unless it is kept firmly under control by pruning, clipping and training. Planting and ornament should march together in tandem from the outset.

ELEMENTS

The options and opportunities for ornament in the garden are limitless: almost everything that is functional in design terms also has decorative possibilities. It is worth exploring the ornamental potential of all the different elements that contribute to the garden's permanent structure, from the ground – paths and paving – up through the means of division and enclosure – hedges, walls and fencing, and gateways – to water features and buildings, whether potting sheds or dog kennels, as well as fixed plant supports, containers and furniture.

What could have been a mundane area on which to park a car has been transformed into a decorative, but useful, forecourt with a labyrinth of setts and gravel whose circular lines are echoed in the clipped box topiary.

If you can afford to do so, it is of course far easier to carry out structural work before planting begins. But if you have a restricted budget, my advice is to spend it initially on what will be immediately noticeable and then constantly review the situation, doing what you can when means allow. Many of our paths at The Laskett, for example, remained as grassy walks for over a decade, and were only paved piecemeal. Equally, if you inherit a garden, never blindly accept what is there; you could revamp a run-of-the-mill path, for instance, by lifting and re-laying one section in an interesting pattern with good materials. Flexibility and pragmatism are essential in garden making: over the years plants grow, and your ideas and budget may change. Always keep an open mind and a fresh eye.

Logic always tells me to begin on the ground, although what can be achieved at that level is less obviously spectacular than the vertical elements. Paths and paving make important contributions to the garden picture, however, delineating and dividing it into areas for different purposes at ground level. Of course they are about moving people and things through the garden, but they also etch in vista and indicate when to pause. They are not the only means of enlivening the ground. Knots and parterres decorate it with sculpted plant matter, and water, whether in the form of a trickling rill, a canal or pond, brings movement and reflections. The aim in using any of these is to produce pattern and a range of colours and textures to enrich the experience of walking around the garden.

When you begin to think of possible materials and treatments I would counsel relating them tonally to the house and, in a small area, having only one section that is complicated. That section should be placed either where it will be most noticed by those on foot and those looking down from an upstairs window, or where it comes as a surprise, perhaps hidden round a corner. Do not set up a conflict between the planting and the paving. A mosaic or 'carpet' pattern of pebbles,

A highly imaginative ground-level pattern, a chequerboard of squares of clipped dwarf box alternating with squares of pebbles, is further personalized by picking out initials within the pebbles. This treatment treads a fine line between a paved area and a parterre.

for instance, calls for restrained planting as a frame. If you place it cheek by jowl with a complex flower border, the result can be a visual war. Elaborate borders are almost always best displayed against greensward or neutral monochrome paving.

In planning or altering paving, other gardens are some of the best sources of ideas: I always take a camera and snap anything interesting. Builders are rendered silent when presented with a photograph of something which, if described to them in words, they will usually pronounce impossible. It is also worth making use of some of the vast number of garden reference books that give repertories of pattern for the different materials that you could use: setts, stone, reconstituted stone, decking, concrete paviours, pebbles, coloured gravels and stone chippings and every kind of brick. Also acquire samples of materials which appeal to you and lay them out on the ground to see what they look like at different times of day and when they are wet. And do consider the possibility of decorative edging, such as up-ended brick placed at a diagonal or Victorian rope tiling, which can add instant style to an existing dull path. You must also decide whether you want a finish where the stress is on ageing and weathering, perhaps with plants creeping up between the crevices, or where the surface must be regularly cleaned to preserve the pristine pattern.

Bitter experience has taught me never to economize on paving. These surfaces receive such a beating from the tramp of feet not to mention laden wheelbarrows, even worse in a smaller than a larger area, that unless they are properly laid with substantial foundations they will start to disintegrate and crumble within only a few years. It is money well spent to have paths professionally laid with foundations of about half a metre (eighteen inches) in depth incorporating a layer of tough plastic to obliterate weeds, hard core and sand below the surface paving components. Whatever the aesthetic merits of paving, its primary purpose must be to be comfortable underfoot.

Changes of level are one of the most exciting elements in any garden's structure. Even one step signals a shift in mood, of moving from one space to another, and ornament is one of the best ways to draw attention to it. Steps can be classic with

balustrading; or rustic in brick or stone; or primitive with wooden boards or logs carving the earth into steps, and edged with larch-pole handrails. They can be left simple and low-key, or dramatized by being flanked either with pairs of urns, finials, stone balls or statues, or by plants, like fastigiate yews or clipped topiary. If you have several steps running to a flight, you have a major garden feature open to every sort of treatment. The greatest extravaganza is a zigzagging or curving double staircase. Such an enterprise would require the services of an architect, but in small gardens, steps are generally far more modest.

Working from the ground up, hedges and their hard-surface equivalents – walls and fences – come next, leading the eye and delineating areas of the garden vertically in the way that paths and paving do at ground level, and providing the means to enclose the garden. Together with paths they form the basic architectural framework and are the test of a well-designed garden. They provide the setting and background for what we normally categorize as ornament, but can themselves be ornamental, adding extra dimensions of colour and texture.

OPPOSITE Set within an otherwise unremarkable gravel pathway, a commissioned mosaic of a lobster becomes the focal point for this secluded area of a seaside garden. It has been given extra emphasis with a seat from which it can be comfortably viewed.

ABOVE All kinds of material can be pressed into service to introduce pattern, texture and colour on the ground. These two examples show that, what is more, the materials need not be expensive (though they should be frost-resistant): recycled broken tiles and ceramics, pebbles or odd discarded objects that have a flat surface are all possibilities. Even a small area treated in this way, placed at a strategic point, can provide unexpected and quite original ornament in a garden.

Let me begin with division achieved through planting, for hedges are one of the few elements in garden planning that cannot be left until later if you are to enjoy their benefits to the full. Evergreen hedges offer by far the greater range of ornamental possibilities. These hedges can be of box, holly, laurel, cupressus and thuja varieties as well as *Lonicera nitida* but the undoubted queen of hedges is yew. It is by no means as

BELOW Layering divisions can be extremely effective. Here a young yew hedge is being trained to form a porthole providing a view to the house, which is glimpsed through a second living fence – a screen of closely clipped hornbeam.

OPPOSITE Hedges are normally used for dividing a garden into rooms, to give protection to the plants within or for creating corridors or walkways to guide the visitor. Used in that way, they can be made into living ornaments by being sculpted by shears. Here they have also been utilized for their potential as living ornament to become the focal point of a large area of grass and low flower beds. Four layers of yew have been deliberately cut to form an abstract sculpture undulating at the top like the waves of the sea, their sophisticated layering casting dramatic shadows.

slow-growing as is often thought and, with proper attention and feeding, will rise about thirty centimetre (a foot) a year. Yew hedges do not necessarily have to be the vast bastions we see in country house gardens. Yew is an extremely accommodating plant. No other, apart from box, responds so well to the shears; you can cut it back brutally or train it into almost any shape you want from buttresses to swags and crenellations, not to mention the range of possibilities for decorative finials. You can also cut windows in a yew hedge that allow you to peer from one part of the garden to the next. And no other hedge sets off sculpted and architectural ornaments better.

Box can be similarly used, the coarser varieties growing as high as yew but over a far longer period of time. In the main its use is better confined to low hedging for edges and for parterres and small topiary work. Hollies can be articulated but only simply, because their leaves are wrinkled and large. Holly is also slow-growing, but none the less a mature holly hedge cut into an interesting profile is a magnificent sight, especially in winter when it is covered in berries.

Whereas evergreen hedges offer firm division and year-long control of vision, deciduous hedges become transparent in winter. That is part of their attraction, and few things are more beautiful than a beech hedge in late winter, with its leaves, a caramel rust colour, still clinging to the branches. Hornbeam is an alternative, although its leaves vanish with the wind in winter. Beech and hornbeam also make excellent low hedges from which you can let finials arise. But the decorative effects to be obtained with deciduous hedging material can only be of the boldest in comparison with the complexities possible with yew or box. Do not ignore the possibilities of what is called a tapestry hedge, which is a mixture of evergreen and deciduous plants with different-coloured foliage, such as beech, field maple and golden privet.

LEFT Enclosing one area of a garden invests it with an unaccountable sense of mystery. Here a basic, concrete-rendered wall has been visually electrified through the dazzling sunshine yellow of the paint, and the entrance given emphasis by a simple archway, its curve made into a circle by the gate below.

RIGHT This length of rendered walling painted a brilliant yellow is all that this garden needs to establish its vibrant identity. Its angular shape and emphasis on the horizontal contrasts with the rugged undulations of the mountain range beyond. The wall would, of course, need to be regularly painted to preserve its pristine freshness as a background to bold foliage and flower planting.

Although the top of a hedge can only be articulated when it reaches the height you wish, its architectural form should be decided before planting. A flat-sided hedge can be very dull in comparison with one with buttresses, pilasters or other excrescences. These interesting shapes are enlivened, in the same way as the façade of a building, by the changing light as sun moves across the garden. It requires little effort when planting to outline the eventual pattern either with paving materials or by cutting shapes into the turf. But do not ignore the possibilities of re-cutting an existing hedge – almost the first thing I did at The Laskett was to crenellate an old thuja hedge – but do check that the plant will survive such radical treatment.

The hard-surface options for enclosure and division range from handsome, if hugely expensive, walls in stone or brick to every variety of fencing, trellis and railing, and all have decorative possibilities. But how do you start?

Lucky are those with boundary walls of brick or stone. If the surface of the wall is dull, it can be enlivened with decorative treillage, or with ceramic tiles or mosaic, or be painted an interesting colour. If the walls are not high enough, they can be raised with trellis or open-work fencing, which can be painted a good colour and act as a plant support. An existing wall can also be provided with a decorative accent, such as a water feature, a plaque or relief, placed to draw the eye.

Even a boundary of close-board fencing, which barely accords privacy, has decorative potential. It can also be painted or stained, or superimposed with colourful trellis screening and a combination of evergreen and flowering climbers.

Within the garden proper there are opportunities for every kind of division – low or high, solid or transparent. Arches in multiples side by side create an arcade. Placed in a continuing row behind each other they form a tunnel. A single one can make an entrance and frame a vista. Pillars with overhead supports will make a pergola.

Trellis and open woodwork panels can divide one part of a garden from another. In virtually every instance they can, unlike hedges, act as plant supports. Such features can also be painted and therefore add splashes of colour other than that of flowers to the garden scene. For beginners with a modest budget I strongly recommend readily available hardwood lattice trellis. It does not last for ever, but for about ten years it gives real value. Painted an interesting colour and cut to shape, lattice trellis is an immortal in the garden design repertory; it was a feature of Roman gardens, and today is available in a variety of meshes and in panels of every size and shape, enabling you to piece together an idiosyncratic composition.

Other options for divisions made of wood range from picket fencing, the history of which goes back to medieval gardens, to Japanese bamboo screening. There are innumerable variations on the picket fence – palings with pointed or profiled heads nailed on to rails at top and bottom and usually painted – and few features are more delightful for delineating a front garden or potager. Wattle fencing also goes back to the middle ages; it has never changed its appearance and offers a robust form of screening for a country garden. Low open-board fences, which appeared in Renaissance gardens and were adapted in response to the Chinoiserie impulses prevalent in the mid-eighteenth century, can make a strong statement in any garden. Painted or

stained a bright colour, and with striking geometric repeat patterns, they make a startling contrast to informal planting. Rustic fences, making use of the natural branches of trees and shrubs with the bark still attached, came into fashion in the Romantic era when they were made into patterns that varied from the highly complex, which could take the form of pointed Gothic arches or repeat patterns in lozenges or diamonds, to rudimentary paling. Today the sophisticated designs can be copied by professionals, although simple screens, pergolas and arches made from inexpensive larch poles are within the abilities of any competent do-it-yourself enthusiast.

Transparent, *claire voyée,* screens can also be made of more durable materials. Built of brick, these make handsome features, far preferable to the pierced concrete sections which are the staple of most garden centres. Firms that specialize in reconstituted stone offer even more elegant forms of low screening, in styles ranging from ever-popular classical

OPPOSITE The rocky edge of a garden escarpment, overlooking a rustic landscape, has been given an appropriately rough-hewn timber fence entirely in character with the terrain.

CENTRE Decorating a wall in a garden is done all too rarely. Here a swirling Gaudiesque ceramic mosaic, filled with vibrant movement and colour, has been applied to a large expanse of brick wall, giving the garden an excitement and sense of energy. *Trompe l'oeil* painting or low-relief sculpture could achieve something of the same effect.

ABOVE A beautifully made frame and an ingenious use of mirror glass do wonders both to disguise a dull wall and enlarge the perceived space in the garden. Softened by clever planting, eight pieces of mirror glass, placed at angles to resemble a folding screen, reflect different facets of the garden. There are many ways of utilizing mirrors in the garden. At ground level they can be used to double the apparent size of a flower bed or, suspended in a gloomy corner, to twinkle in the darkness as they catch the light.

Splendid architectural treillage used to stunning effect as a transparent wall is given extra interest by the addition of mirror glass, placed so that the eye cannot immediately distinguish between reflection and the view through the fretwork. The winter months bring a startling contrast between the angular geometry of the treillage and the intricate tracery of the branches behind it. In the winter months too the colour of the painted treillage comes into its own against a predominantly monochrome background.

balustrading to Jacobean and Victorian baroque. Low walls offer superb planting opportunities and, because they are often sited to contain a terrace next to the house, those are to be welcomed. But don't let climbers so engulf the screening that the rhythm of its architecture becomes obscured.

Metal screening and railings provide yet more options for ornamental divisions. A huge repertory of eighteenth- and nineteenth-century-style ironwork is available, but don't overlook the possibilities of designing something unique yourself. It is surprisingly inexpensive to commission a local craftsman. Architectural salvage yards often have runs of old railing or panels of decorative ironwork that can be used on their own or incorporated into something new. If you intend to have plants climbing over the metal screens, be warned that metal can become scorching hot in summer sun and deadly chill in winter frost, and some plants are not happy struggling with these extremes.

Gates, like screening, can either offer us tantalizing glimpses of what lies beyond them, or deny us that sight by being firmly shut and solid. Although a gate's basic purpose is utilitarian – to keep animals and people out – or at least to signal that whoever opens it is about to trespass unless invited, a gate also gives the psychological message that one is about to cross a boundary into something hidden and secret. In the physical act of swinging open and stepping through an outside gate, one moves out of the public domain into a private world. The effect may be less if the gate is inside a garden, but the frisson of admission still pertains.

All these subliminal overtones give the garden planner every reason to make the most of gates. Even in a small garden, I would try and find a place for one. It could either form part of a screen or wall that divides the space into two sections or, as a solid door, stand as the culmination of a short vista, a prop to conceal the boundary of the garden, where its presence will cause the viewer to imagine more space beyond the gate. Even the simplest of mass-manufactured metal or wooden gates can be dressed up. At the very least they can be painted an interesting colour. More, they can be flanked by supports or piers with finials at the top or set within an arch of even the most rudimentary sort which, in its turn, can support an embroidery of fragrant and pretty climbers. Gate piers in stone, brick or reconstituted stone offer some of the best pedestals that I know for the display of a pair of decorative finials. Rampant lions, sphinxes, winged eagles, urns, vases, pineapples or simple balls are just some of the ready repertory. But why not be inventive? I have seen large ballcocks, intended for domestic plumbing, painted and used. The glazed ceramic pumpkins available at garden centres would also make original finials.

If you can, make the top of the piers finish above eye level. When lifted to stand silhouetted against the sky, any ornament makes a spectacular impact. In fact, you should use any opportunity to raise ornament. Too few people think about doing this – it is not an exercise for the timid, but when it is bravely done the result can be electrifying.

Gates themselves come in every form, and can be wholly or partially solid or transparent. Of wood, metal or simulated metal, recycled, ready- or custom-made, they can be finished in every kind of paint effect, and touches gilded to catch the light.

If I had to select one ornamental feature which would give the most unequivocal identity to a garden, it would be some kind of built structure, whether a summerhouse, treehouse, pavilion, temple, tower, grotto, gazebo, aviary, dovecote, arbour or folly. Although they can be expensive, if you have space to build one in your garden I would argue that it would be a worthwhile investment, because it will allow you to make the boldest statement of individual style and personal taste. The form it takes is limited only by your imagination and pocket.

If the point of departure is the decorative potential, the building can also have a more useful function – to work, sit or eat in, to act in part as a store or toolshed, to be a changing room for a pool, or to accommodate tender plants that need to spend the winter under cover. Or it can perform multiple roles. All of this should be given thought before any purchase is made or commission given. As well as style and function, you should consider scale and placing. Particular care should be given to these if it is to be near your house. Study the disposition of the existing planting in the immediate surroundings, working out what can be sacrificed while still leaving an attractive framework of trees and shrubs to set off the new building. The erection of anything beyond the simplest of arbours will almost

LEFT An imposing castellated brick gateway enclosing a glazed wooden door with gothic tracery is a splendid way of dressing up an entrance. The tracery and the crenellation add touches of medieval romance to what would otherwise be a utilitarian garden gate. The two simple steps up add a note of expectancy, as does the partial glimpse of what lies beyond. The flanking beech hedge needs to be cut back to reveal all the architectural detail clearly.

RIGHT A custom-made gate in the form of a trophy of garden tools makes an inviting entrance to a grassy walk. Designed by George Carter, it marks both a divide and an invitation to pass through and continue towards the stone obelisk topped by a gilded ball. The hedges are clearly young and still being trained, but that fact only emphasizes the major role ornament can play in the initial stages of garden making. Perhaps a little gilded detailing on the tools might better link the gate to the obelisk beyond.

certainly require the services of a professional builder, and perhaps may need planning permission.

If you already have a garden building but it is not to your liking, rather than demolishing or replacing it – especially if it is solidly or expensively built – give some thought as to how you might change its appearance. It is amazing what a lick of paint and some extra decoration can achieve. Could you apply columns or pilasters to the façade or attach gingerbread fretwork to the eaves? Would the addition of trellis to the walls give it the visual articulation it lacks? If the foundations are sturdy enough, would a new shape of roof with a decorative finial endow it with interest?

A garden building often requires as much maintenance as a house. Roofs and drainage require vigilant attention. Readily available prefabricated structures seem to have obsolescence built into them from the day of arrival. If made of wood, the structure will need regular painting and, as time goes by, the replacing of joists and timbers as these rot and disintegrate. That is why more solid building materials are a better long-term investment. But even these are subject to crumbling mortar and the incursion of damp. But all the effort is worth it, especially if the building is the only major decorative statement in your garden. A building signals a human presence in the garden; it can also pull a disparate composition together and draw the eye

OPPOSITE, FAR LEFT With the aid of a builder there is no reason why the enchanting effect of this airborne building could not be achieved with easily available ingredients. A ready-made garden shed could be given custom-made doors and windows, lifted on to a sturdy platform surrounded by simple fencing and accessed by a flight of wooden steps. This is a hugely imaginative treatment of what, at ground level, might have been an unremarkable building, and an object lesson in how to dress up the commonplace through painted detail, siting and good planting.

OPPOSITE, TOP RIGHT Utilitarian features can make decorative contributions to the garden. Here, what could have been a workaday chicken coop, hardly deserving a glance, has been transformed into a pretty, elevated building giving delight to an otherwise unalleviated stretch of trees and grass.

OPPOSITE, BOTTOM RIGHT The strong sinuous lines and plain colour of this well-placed arbour make a fine contrast to the lavish herbaceous flower border in which it is set.

RIGHT A tiny grotto has been lined inside with shells collected from the beach and given a stained-glass window rescued from a demolition site. The brilliant deployment of the window at the level of the water of the pond outside gives the visitor an almost fairy-tale experience.

A delicate metal canopy with art nouveau detailing makes its own statement in the winter months, while in summer, when it is spangled with leaf and flower, its lines are obscured. Perfectly framing a life-size statue at a crossing, it makes a traditional country garden tableau in the classic mode. Low hedges and clipped vertical accents in box and yew give architectural order to the richly planted borders and baroque curves of the statue.

away from haphazard planting; it will be something delightful to look at all through the year and may be really useful as well.

Many structures in a garden end up as plant supports, but there are others whose role is solely to do precisely that. These constructions can resemble buildings whose roofs, walls and doors have been removed, leaving the supporting framework over which the plants may clamber. Pergolas, arcades and arbours can be made in styles that run the whole gamut of the historical and contemporary repertory, and can be as severe or

as decorative as you wish. If you opt for wood, why not paint the supports a bold colour and add some finials? If you go for brick pillars, why not make patterns in the columns with different-coloured bricks? If you opt for a reconstituted stone classical colonnade, think about a colour wash. Let your fantasy run riot. Construct something around a salvaged window or door frame. Best of all, commission something original in wood or metal: don't be afraid to be bold or to shock – a wigwam or even a geodesic dome is as valid as a gothic arcade.

Wooden shafts support a higgledy-piggledy double canopy of latticework to form an eccentric pergola for a wisteria. An essay in the joys of improvisation, such an inspired construction is a reminder that superb garden effects can be cobbled together from the cheapest materials. Anyone who saw this would never quite forget it. Much is gained from its juxtaposition with an abstract arrangement of tightly clipped box balls.

If embarking on a building is expensive and demanding in terms of maintenance, bringing water into the garden is even more so, at least if it is on any scale beyond the elementary filling of a small container to act as a *miroir d'eau*. A single deep stone trough or half barrel filled with clean water and placed to reflect other ornaments or plants or simply the changing skies can be an extremely elegant garden ornament. But for anything more elaborate, I would like to send up a sharp warning flare. Even the simplest of fountains need annual servicing. In all areas that experience more than a degree or two of frost, they have to be emptied and cleaned before the winter and, for safety's sake, bagged until spring. Through long experience I am only too well aware that water calls for eternal vigilance. I returned home once to find the top bowl of a fountain as a heap of shattered fragments. Cold had frozen the rainwater that had collected in the bowl causing it to expand with the inevitable result. That fountain is one of the great adornments to our garden and its spring filling, when jets of clear water shoot skywards once again, is for us one of the magic moments in the garden year. But achieving what seems so simple an effect requires energy and commitment. Everything that could go wrong, from the main basin leaking through the mortar to the collapse of the pump, continues to occur.

Nor are water features easy to install in the first place. Do not be seduced by the garden centre into believing that you merely dig an irregular hole, plonk in one of their plastic liners, fill it with water, pop in a few aquatic plants and fish, and that is it. It is not. (A particular *caveat* about fish: the chances are, especially if you live in the country, that by having these you will merely be feeding the local cat population and the passing heron.) Nevertheless, I would not be without water in the garden. Symbol of life and nourishment, it brings movement and the refraction of light into the smallest space. Its beauty as part of the garden scene is unique. As long as you have taken on board the complications involved, you will be able to cope.

In a tiny urban garden, water is far more effective when confined to a small, easily maintained feature, such as a wall fountain. This, the classic *bocca*, comes in any number of styles from grottoesque, in a traditional form such as a stone mask, to minimalist, using sleek stainless-steel chutes. It can either

This breathtakingly romantic composition makes the most of an existing pond, the presence of water and the views to the countryside beyond. Such a vision is not easily achieved. It calls for the presence of water in the garden at the outset and the services of a landscape architect able to re-fashion what is there into such a desirable composition, constructing the decking walkway, the viewpoint with its containing rail, as well as supervising what is hugely complex marginal planting. Such spectacles present ongoing maintenance problems, the least of which is keeping the paintwork pristine, which must be taken on board from the beginning.

figure as an ornamental incident, for instance on a terrace, or as the focal point of a vista. Teamed with appropriate planting in or near the basin, few garden ornaments are more attractive. If they are situated low on the wall, they can also be built up by adding rocks and architectural pieces around the water source. Another feature suitable for small gardens is the boulder pierced so that water merely bubbles up through and over it, its basin and pump hidden below the surface. It can be placed as a focal point or among shady, damp loving ferns as a mysterious surprise. All that is required to install the simpler features is a source of electricity at the site and a means of concealing the submersible pump that recycles the water.

Water on any larger scale is, of course, magnificent, whether it is a rill – a trickle of water made to meander or to run in a straight line through the garden – or a substantial fountain, waterfall, large pond or canal. However, designing and installing such things is the province of the professional designer and is hugely costly, especially if you do not have a water source in your garden. If you are lucky enough to have a natural stream or brook running through the garden, or have an old fish or cattle pond that could be pressed into service, then you should exploit its full ornamental potential. Throw a bridge across the stream and make it decorative both in its architecture and colour. Whether it is rustic or oriental, zinging yellow or sombre blue, strictly minimalist or frothily Victorian, it could be covered, or embellished with gate piers, or even have a pavilion in the centre. And don't ignore the charm of stepping stones.

Sheets of water provide opportunities for displays of water lilies and flowering marginals but also, just as importantly, for reflections: a centrepiece of any static, strong vertical like a statue works wonders, but a mobile, such as a revolving sphere or a tree with fluttering metallic leaves, would be sensational.

Apart from a building, one single, striking hard-surface ornament, such as a statue or an obelisk, is the shortest cut to individualizing a garden that I know. A reproduction Victorian sundial in the middle of a rose garden, for example, gives out a very different message from an oversized stone artichoke in a vegetable garden, while an eccentric salvaged object is immediately intriguing, arousing questions about what prompted its presence.

OPPOSITE, FAR LEFT The simplest of fountains has been made of stones threaded on to the pipe from which water gushes out at the summit. The stones have been carefully chosen for their texture and colour when wet.

OPPOSITE, CENTRE The moveable accent of a painted metal bird has been wittily placed to enjoy the plashing water of a fountain.

OPPOSITE, RIGHT An ingenious minute wall fountain, a tier of funnels, produces the effect of a miniature cascade.

LEFT A spectacular, but not overly grand, cascade like this calls for professional construction on a site with a steep change of level. The visual impact is ravishing but the means of attaining it relatively simple: a series of stone steps and shallow pools falling one into the other with large stones laid as bridges. The detailing of the risers to the steps achieves a series of decorative and quite complicated small waterfalls. Of course having a natural water source would be a major advantage, but the same effect could be achieved by pumping the water around.
The luscious marginal planting enhances what would be a major set piece in any garden.

Hard-surface fixed accents run the gamut of those within the classical inherited tradition, including sundials, urns, bird baths, statues, vases, well-heads, finials and obelisks, to those more of our own time, found and salvaged pieces, items which can range from an old telephone kiosk to pieces of abandoned industrial or farming machinery. Whatever your decision, my general advice would be to have only one, or a pair, if you are using it as a focal point in a small area where it can be seen at a glance. If you have a larger garden with divisions that obscure the view from one area into the next, you can treat each compartment differently.

But fixed accents need not necessarily be made only of hard, inanimate material: evergreen ornament in the form of topiary can be used for any number of delightful effects. If you intend to try your hand at topiary, buy one of the many books available on the subject. Essentially, all it calls for is patience while the plant grows and the skill to cut it into the shape you want.

ABOVE A combination of hard-surface and living fixed accents – a statue on a plinth flanked by a low box hedge and box spirals – in a traditional, classic formula exudes the calm authority of centuries of western garden making.

RIGHT An elegant sundial in the eighteenth-century style at the centre of this nostalgic garden holds the cross-axes together in a timeless classic formal composition of a rectangle or square quartered. The clipped mopheads and hedges demonstrate the fine borderline which exists between hard-surface ornament and topiary, while the pattern and the textures of the paths add ground-level interest.

But to establish immediate identity you need to draw on the large variety of ready-trained topiary available from specialist nurseries and good garden centres. Such pieces are not cheap, but you can set the cost against the fact that their effect on a garden is all the more startlingly instant for representing years of growth and careful training. (Do check the suitability of your soil conditions, however, before you splash out.) The most commonly seen shapes are standards, balls, cones, pyramids and corkscrews; in addition, there is the occasional whimsical figure, such as a rabbit or a peacock, and, reflecting recent trends, shrubs given 'cloud clipping' in the oriental manner. Two box cones will dress up the entrance to a garden path. Multiply them along the path and you have a mini stately avenue guiding the eye along it. Place four yew balls at the corners of a rectangle or square of paving and you have signalled a piazza. Do the same with four standard golden privet at the angles of an intersection of two paths and with a hard-surface ornament added to the centre, the result is a major centrepiece for an entire garden.

Just as existing dull buildings can be improved or even transformed into ornamental delights, so there are many plants that you may already have that could be trained and clipped into stunning fixed accents. Radical topiary is one way of taming a plant that you might otherwise chop down. A yew, even the size

of a tree, can be drastically re-cut without any ill effects and will cheerfully spring again. Cut the outline of the shape you want, say a sugar loaf, and within a few years the spaces will fill out with new growth. Holly and beech are other shrubs that can be subjected to the shears and turned into architectural shapes, such as a ball or drum.

Seats can make fixed or moveable accents: the options they present for use in a garden's composition are almost limitless. In permanent positions they can either form a welcoming climax to a walk, or be placed to view a panorama, or be tucked away to be discovered on a tour through the garden. They should always be inviting, indicating that you can sit upon them

OPPOSITE A pair of obelisks provide an immediate contrast of surface and shape among the predominantly leafy green surroundings. Obelisks in reconstituted stone are part of the stock-in-trade of garden ornament suppliers but these have been specially constructed, making clever use of simple paving slabs and flints embedded into cement.

BELOW Massive piers of clipped sorbus act as permanent sentinels in what is otherwise a sprawling, informally planted garden, adding much-needed vertical elements and structure. Topiary is a far cheaper means of achieving this effect than using hard-surface materials, but does demand the patience to wait for growth as well as the effort to train and maintain the shape. Other hedging plants including beech, which has the advantage of retaining its leaves in winter, or evergreens could be used.

LEFT A permanent seat has been woven out of willow to encompass the base of an old tree, making a statement about natural materials as well as providing a handsome focal point. The addition of the suspended platform, also made out of willow, for feeding birds again draws the eye. In an informal country garden virtually no other ornaments would be needed beyond these.

RIGHT The fact that the table and benches are immoveable ensures the perfection of this composition, which is neatly delineated by mophead acacias at the four corners of the paved area. What we see could be a scheme for an entire small garden. The same elements in a moveable form would only be untidy. The deliberate use of rough, hardly hewn wood, keeps the style of the garden unpretentious and accessible. The same elements in stone or reconstituted stone would tilt the composition towards classical grandeur.

and, when sat upon, they should also present the eye with something to ravish it. In addition, they offer the ideal place from which to enjoy fragrant planting. If the seat is to play a star role, forming a climax to a scheme or tableau, it needs to be given extra prominence, for instance enhanced with flanking architectural features or framed by a flower-decked arch or arbour. If it is to play merely a supporting role, a minor incident, it is better left understated. In both form and function, seats are very versatile – the right style in the right place can enhance the mood and geometry of a formal garden as much as a different kind can emphasize the sweet disorder of a natural glade. Remember that unless they are made of stone, seats usually have to be taken in or protected during winter.

Appealing though they are, it is better not to overpopulate a small garden with too many fixed seats. The result can be municipal and confused. Moveable, lightweight or folding seats are another matter. They can be seized and placed anywhere that you wish to sit and enjoy the garden for a while and then put away. But you should not ignore the decorative possibilities of these either. Seats of this kind are available in a bewildering number of styles. My advice is to keep them simple, stick to plain or neutral colours and avoid patterned fabrics.

Containers are as versatile as portable garden furniture and, like the furniture, can be functional or purely ornamental. They are the foot soldiers of ornament: when planted up they can be deployed in all sorts of situations, rescuing a failing scheme at an instant. Planted for different seasons and positioned so that they form patterns or informal groups, they present a kaleidoscope of decorative possibilities. Their only drawback is maintenance: they are extremely labour-intensive and if your aim is minimum input do not attempt them, for all you will end up with is a sad display of ailing or dead plants.

But why plant them at all? Many are so handsome that they can be placed as eye-catchers and incidents in their own right. There are so many types, shapes and sizes now available, from reconstituted stone vases to lustrously coloured glazed clay pots. Pop a sizeable one in a border to make a contrast of shape and colour, or place a row of smaller ones on a shelf. Or fill some with mounds of stones or coloured pebbles.

Portable plant supports, though serving a practical use, can also be highly decorative in themselves. A huge variety, ranging from sturdy, beautifully finished hardwood obelisks to swirling steel spirals or prettily plaited willow cones, can be bought off the shelf. Even simple stakes can be dressed up by being painted all the colours of the rainbow and having pretty finials, such as a ball or pineapple or even a sea shell, added to the top. Such ornaments can either form an integral part of the structure of a garden border, especially when they are used to add height among low-growing plants, or be moved around at will to add small notes of colour or wit.

Plant supports and containers are just two components of the small garden magician's conjuring kit. In recent years the essence of a garden's style and identity has become increasingly more often expressed through moveable ornament – artefacts which can, as it were, be produced out of a hat, picked up and moved at will, changing the mood of the garden as often and as

quickly as the owner wishes. These kind of items were not absent in gardens in the past, but it is only now that they seem to be coming into their own. To be portable, they must, of course, be reasonably small or lightweight and therefore relatively inexpensive, and this makes them particularly suited to small gardens. Their relationship to the interior decoration of the house is also becoming increasingly apparent, particularly in spaces that are, in effect, extensions of the house.

The development of moveable ornament is summed up in the tablescape, a surface that supports what can only be described as a seasonal still life. In winter it could be an arrangement of beautiful stones encircling a container with a clipped evergreen. Spring might bring pots of tulips and trophies of shells and summer an arrangement of craft pottery. Autumn may present a display of golden, ochre and orange pumpkins and squashes along with arrangements of twigs and branches. With careful thought and a sure eye there is no end

FAR LEFT A single well-crafted pot with generous curves and subtle glazes is always welcome as an ornament. It can have a myriad uses: here it acts in concert with the clipped low box hedge to give strength and firm line and a note of longevity to luxuriantly planted borders.

CENTRE Plant containers, as long as they are frostproof, can add to the garden picture in winter. Here eight oversized terracotta pots have been placed to make an orderly pattern within a bed. Who knows but in spring they may be moved elsewhere. Placing containers of plants in beds can be incredibly useful during the flowering season too, filling gaps and adding interest where it has flagged.

ABOVE Placed on the edge of a placid, waterlily-decked pool, a collection of flowering plants in pots brings a duplication of bloom through reflection. The eye-catching blue and white globes belong to agapanthus, of which many types are particularly suited to containers because they are tender and need to be taken in and sheltered over winter. Once the flowers are over, these pots can be moved out of such important positions and replaced with other seasonal plants. Natural rock stepping stones add to the complex, romantic mood, which is epitomized by the transient reflections.

These are three variations on a theme that is very much a feature of contemporary small gardens: the tablescape – an alfresco still life. All sorts of found objects and bric-a-brac, not to mention plants in containers, can be pressed into service to form a pleasing arrangement, and can then be re-formed countless times through the year. Tablescapes are intensely personal statements reflecting both the eye and the interests of the arranger. Their modest domestic scale is particularly appropriate to the small garden; and, according to the role they are to play, they can be sited almost anywhere. They can be tucked into a leafy shrub border as a quiet incident, or be placed in a prime, eye-catching position on a terrace.

to the permutations of tableaux to be achieved. Similar displays can be situated elsewhere in the garden, on pedestals or shelves on the outside walls of the house or on a shed – parades of terracotta pots or other modest collectables like cloches, discarded pressed-glass bottles or old pottery jars. Venerable old garden implements like forks, hoes and spades can be given an honourable retirement displayed on a sheltered wall. Old metal watering cans can placed almost anywhere to catch the eye and evoke nostalgia for past times.

Cut-outs are typical of the new carefree approach to ornament. Made of metal or well-treated timber, they can range

from *trompe l'oeil* renderings of grand architectural or sculptural features placed as major focal points to colourful images of life-size nibbling rabbits, predatory cats or chirping birds. Whole cut-out figures may be of classical statues – *folies de grandeur* of a type you could not afford – placed, tongue-in-cheek, as a major focal point for a response of momentary astonishment, or be more witty than arresting, like a gardener resting on a spade placed in a flower bed.

These types of image add wit to the scene and reflect the idiosyncratic taste of the owners. I remember being entranced by an inscription suspended from branches bidding me to look

ABOVE LEFT One of the great advantages of lightweight accents is that they can be moved according to season as well as to whim. A wire-mesh figure like a ghost which bends forward to pluck a flower from a swathe of tulips in spring could be as aptly placed in a border of annuals later in the summer.

ABOVE RIGHT Two life-size painted cut-outs of geese, sited so that they are reflected in the water, give the pond the waterfowl it lacks.

at what was set before me, and loved seeing a spider's web of fine string threaded with coloured glass beads strung between fencing posts. A dark cranny will spring to life if you hang a witch ball or tiny pieces of mirror glass there. A weather-vane cut into a silhouette to reflect your personal interests will always cause a smile. Modest, simple gestures like these will set all you do apart and will bestow a depth of thought into what is often conceived in the crudest terms as 'design'. Design is superficial, meaning is everything.

The word 'painting' has recurred through these pages for a reason. Not enough thought is given to paint as a source of colour, and hence ornament, in the garden. The old horticultural credo of the Arts and Crafts school was against this kind of colour, always emphasizing that nothing should compete with the palette of nature, and hence recommending shades of green or stained natural timber for any garden artefact. But a garden is artificial from its very conception; even the most seemingly natural of gardens are products of the exercise of artifice. So there is no reason at all to observe that rule. A short excursion into garden history quickly reveals that colour ran riot in the gardens of the past. Fences, for instance, were marbled or painted stone or coral. Finials were gilded. Coats of arms in all their rude primary glory figured on shields borne by heraldic beasts. Statues were polychrome, life-size figures painted like

LEFT Gaily painted posts like barber's poles or those lifted from a Venetian canal mark the corners of beds. They have been placed strategically so that when the garden is being watered, the hose can be moved without fear of damaging the plants. Painted posts in the garden have a distinguished history. Topped by heraldic beasts, they were a feature of the Tudor royal gardens in the sixteenth century. At the close of the following century the flower borders of William III's palace at Het Loo, Holland, had plant supports that were painted blue and topped by golden crowns.

RIGHT The tradition of using brightly coloured and patterned tiles in the garden comes from the Mediterranean and still flourishes today. In the famous tile gardens of Portugal, for instance, all the architectural features, from the benches to the water cisterns, are composed of tiles. Here, hexagonal piers covered in tiles portraying fruit and flowers bring stability, structure, height and brilliant, year-round colour to the garden. In areas with harsh winter climates, there is a danger that the tiles would be destroyed. But a tiled figurative panel that was mounted and so could be taken inside during winter would enliven a garden wall.

waxworks, and deliberately placed to confuse from afar. Arcades and tunnels were painted, with architectural details picked out and enhanced in different shades of the same colour. All this should be an incentive for you to choose a palette for your garden much as you would for a room in your house. And any small garden will be dominated by a view of at least one side of the house, so that too should be drawn in as part of the overall scheme. Indeed, linking the house and garden through colour is one of the foundation stones of a successful small garden.

Although you may find this recommendation surprising, you will be equally astonished to discover how the introduction of colourfully painted artefacts in no way upsets your appreciation of the tonality of bloom. If chosen carefully, the two marry in a highly satisfactory way because nothing can detract from the fact that the overall colour of a garden can never be anything other than green. Colour in paint comes into its own in winter when set against the backdrop of leafless branches and twigs and evergreens.

That plea for the use of paint should not detract from the more traditional role of colour in respect of ornament: the reds and dusky pinks of brick, the buff and creamy hues of stone, the greys and whites of marble, the dusky greys and blues of lead and slate, the verdigris of bronze, the various shades of concrete slabs, the technicolour glazes on ceramic containers, not to mention ubiquitous terracotta. All contribute colour which itself changes with the quality of light.

Does artificial lighting count as part of ornament? I think

FAR LEFT Even unadorned, this intense blue wall would be a powerful statement, making a dramatic background which would lift the most mundane of plantings. Here it supports an arresting polychrome leaf sculpture whose beauty and scale demand space and no competing attraction.

CENTRE An intricate *claire voyée* gate has been given added emphasis and importance by being painted a brilliant blue.

BELOW Two bright blue folding chairs are potent reminders that colour can be introduced into a garden by artefacts as well as plants. Here they are adjuncts to a large shell-bedecked trough that is itself a major ornamental feature.

that it does, although I have never seen a garden satisfactorily lit other than for a party, when it was transformed into a surreal fantasy. Even lighting a small garden is as complicated as lighting a stage set, but more difficult because a garden mutates through the seasons, so it should be done by a professional lighting designer. However, although special cable has to be used, the relatively simple lighting of a hard-surface ornament can be handled by an ordinary qualified electrician. A small tableau shimmering with light would be striking when viewed from the windows of the house at night. You must decide first whether you want it to be sharply pin-pointed by a brilliant spotlight angled from the front or whether you want a softer, far more diffused effect, making it seem that the ornament is emerging mysteriously from the shadows.

Perhaps the most successful lights are those normally used for security immediately around the house. Triggered by infra-red rays, they spring to life as your guests leave at night, suddenly suffusing the garden with a magical aura. This, for me, makes the perfect finale to a memorable evening.

ABOVE What may be a featureless pond during the day has become a scene of dramatic interest at night with the sophisticated deployment of artificial light. Playing up the reflective qualities of the water, several uplights illuminate the pondside plants.

RIGHT A handsome town garden, which already makes use of a sculptural fountain as a focal point, is a spectacular sight in the evening when it is lit like a stage set; but such subtle effects call for the services of an expert to install and maintain.

The twelve gardens that follow were chosen for their originality and contrasting styles and because they demonstrate both the principles and elements of ornament in action. The fact that every garden was made by its designers for themselves (although this only emerged after the selection had been made) is testament to the importance of imposing individual personality rather than merely a 'design solution' on to a garden. I hope that the gardens will be an inspiration as well as a point of departure for those aspiring to make their own personal statement in terms of ornament.

COMPOSITIONS

A NEW TWIST ON TRADITION

OPPOSITE The brilliantly painted dead tree (**1**) has an electrifying effect. It boldly transforms the garden, which is otherwise beautiful in a conventional way, into something far more idiosyncratic. The changes of texture at ground level from gravel to grass and then to brick give the illusion that the space is far larger than the reality. As the sun moves, so do the patterns cast by the tree and the decorative but sturdy treillage (**9**) that divides the garden.

ABOVE A view from a window of the house shows a chequerboard of squares. These are filled mainly with annuals and perennials but one is used for a display of terracotta pots, and another as a miniature *miroir d'eau* (**3**). The containers, chairs and small sculptures add a variety of moveable ornament which can be easily re-sited.

LEFT The formal use of water purely as a mirror for the sky is remarkably effective even on such a small scale.

The garden of the painter and photographer Andrew Lawson and his sculptor wife Bryony occupies just a third of an acre at the back of an old stone house in the Cotswolds. The pressure to create a conventional garden must have been almost overwhelming, for the location and the architecture of the house would seem to call for a romantic cottage garden within the Arts and Crafts tradition with an abundant use of natural materials like stone and wood and a lavish display of traditional herbaceous plants. What is striking has been the owners' ability to marry this repertory from the past with a stunning statement of the present, vividly demonstrating that the two, well handled, can live side by side, each enhancing the other.

What sets this garden apart in terms of ornament is the masterly decision not to fell a flowering cherry tree which had died (**1**) but instead paint it a vibrant blue, immediately endowing the space with a surreal quality. It has an almost magical presence, giving the garden instant originality and identity. (I have seen a dead tree elsewhere treated in a related way: its branches were hung with silver leaves cut out of tin foil, the effect astonishing as it shimmered in the light.) It is an inspirational way to turn a loss into a bonus.

The twisting branches of the tree provide a startling counterpoint to the geometric pattern of square beds, set into the gravel terrace. Each has been treated differently: one is a small pool (**3**), and is brilliantly sited so that the reflection of the tree can be seen from the seating arbour (**5**). Placed to catch the evening sun, the arbour has a sinuous ogee arch that echoes the gothic-style windows of the house and conservatory that look on to it. A treillage screen (**9**), made of the same weathered wood as the arbour, divides the garden and is designed to throw complex shadows across the lawn in winter (see pages 76–7). There are two vistas from the gravel terrace (**A**): one down a path (**6**) paved to exaggerate its false perspective and leading to a *trompe l'oeil* window (**7**) painted on the end wall; the other along a cutting bed punctuated with two handsome wooden plant supports (**8**).

In terms of maintenance the tree requires painting regularly; it needs to be kept pristine in contrast to the other, deliberately weathered, wooden ornaments. The smallness of the beds and the *miroir d'eau* means that keeping these crammed with bulbs and annuals or filled with clean water is not too daunting.

AREAS OF THE GARDEN

A Gravel terrace
B Mixed border
C Alpine pyramid
D Pleached lime avenue
E Cutting bed

ORNAMENTAL FEATURES

1 Painted tree
2 Craft chair
3 *Miroir d'eau*
4 Flagstone with inscription
5 Seating arbour
6 Gravel and granite path
7 *Trompe l'oeil* window
8 Pyramids
9 Treillage screen

OPPOSITE TOP The arbour (**5**) and its comfortable garden bench are true to the Jekyllesque Arts and Crafts tradition, avoiding colour in preference to weathered timber.

OPPOSITE CENTRE Seats need not only be utilitarian. Here a handsome, solid craft piece (**2**), designed by Paul Anderson, has been deliberately placed as a counterfoil to the feathery and ephemeral foliage and flowers, as something interesting to look at. It is made of weathered driftwood. Note the fact that the conservatory window frames are also painted blue, although in a tone far lighter than that of the tree.

OPPOSITE BOTTOM A traditional herringbone brick path runs through the small cutting garden (**E**) that is semi-concealed from the gravel terrace (**A**) by the treillage screen (**9**). It is thickly planted with spring bulbs which will be replaced later by annuals. Two wooden pyramids (**8**), which will support summer-flowering climbers, give permanent, vertical interest, and evergreen clipped box plants supply further year-round accents in the border.

NATURE SCULPTED

OPPOSITE A masterly composition of clipped box, bay, rosemary and other plants frames a beguiling, undulating walkway which moves from one of the garden's stone paths, across the gravel of the main terrace (**C**), and towards the stone terrace (**B**) in front of the house. The shapes are harmonious but vary in height, colour, leaf shape and texture. The large arched doorway acts as a focal point for this vista, but even the colour of paint – like everything else in this garden – melds with the natural colours, including the sky, of the surroundings. The virtual absence of anything deciduous makes this a year-round picture with only subtle variations through the seasons.

ABOVE LEFT Furniture and a fine, transparent wrought-iron gate (**7**) make the most of the view over the escarpment below the terrace. The bare trunk of a standard tree (**6**) adds a strong vertical but the dome of its clipped mophead shape is an aerial echo of the soft mounds of clipped shrubs at ground level.

ABOVE RIGHT While the topiary fuses tonally with the landscape, its clipped, geometric silhouettes make it stand out from the wild surroundings.

LEFT The passage of time has given once-functional artefacts like these stone pestles (**5**) visual fascination worthy of deployment in a garden still life.

It is not often that I bestow the word masterpiece on a garden, but that is an accurate description of this creation by the great French garden designer Nicole de Vésian, who died in 1996. It is the garden she lovingly created around her own house, La Louve, in Provence, which is now cherished and immaculately maintained by the present owner.

It is a large garden spilling around a house built on a hill and thus affording spectacular views to the surrounding landscape. Only one section of the garden is shown here, but it illustrates the principles upon which the whole was conceived and the ways those can be reinterpreted in much smaller spaces.

Three major impulses have formed this exercise in design and ornament. One is the twentieth-century's cult and appreciation of abstract non-figurative form for its own sake. The second is a familiarity with the garden traditions of China and Japan, where the training of trees and shrubs is one of the highest skills of garden art. To that must be added a determination that the garden should respond to the genius of the place, in this instance the calcareous rocks and sparse terrain of Provence with its poor soil and parched summers. The design works from the premise that the cultivated garden should echo the landscape – indeed, that the two should flow effortlessly together.

The built structures are all made of local stone, so that tonally the house, garden walls, paths and paving and containers merge into the countryside beyond. Only tough, resilient plants native to the region have been used: junipers and fruit trees, vines, cistus and hibiscus varieties, bay, box, rosemary, germander, santolina, valerian, rosemary, lavender and irises. Together these make a tapestry of shades and tones from dark, blue-green to pale, silver-grey green enlivened by the juxtaposition of different leaf shapes and textures. The aesthetic delight resides in the complex and subtle rhythms of outline of its numerous clipped shrubs. The lesson here is about creating ornament from living plant material which, besides being a background for setting off the hard-surface artefacts, is also an echo and replication of the shapes those artefacts make. These are rarely more complicated than stone balls, architectural fragments, a cattle trough (**4**), low walls around trees. These are all man-made but seem to unfold naturally from the terrain.

This is the kind of garden that depends on the improvisatory powers and eye of its designer. It is wholly asymmetrical and consists of walks or vistas that meander along paths of stone or gravel, pause, move up or down steps, making visitors conscious at every turn of the shapes that fall on the eye and of the landscape beyond. This is living ornament of extraordinary perfection. But such beauty is demanding for, in order to keep it pristine, it demands year-round attention to absolutely every single detail.

AREAS OF THE GARDEN

A The belvedere
B Flagstone terrace outside the house
C Gravel terrace in front of the summer kitchen
D Barbecue area

ORNAMENTAL FEATURES

1 Metal gate
2 Tiered topiary tree
3 Dining furniture
4 Stone trough
5 Still life of stone pestles
6 Topiary mophead
7 Wrought-iron gate
8 Stone bench
9 Barbecue bench with 'window'

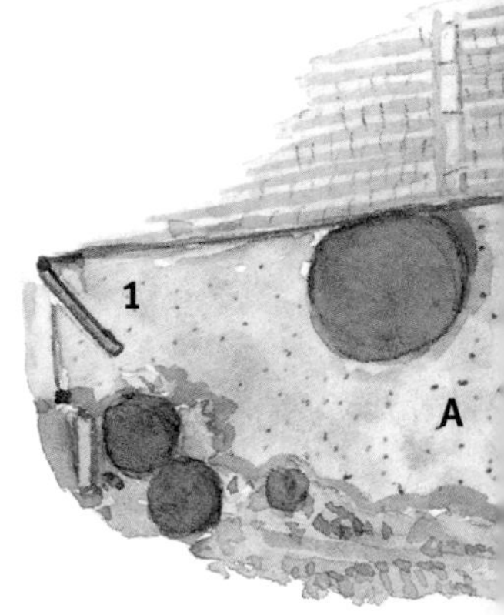

OPPOSITE, LEFT The strong but lightweight metal furniture (**3**) is designed to stay out of doors most of the year. The area is made more intimate by being contained on three sides by the house, and by two walls, which are low enough for diners to enjoy uninterrupted views of the Luberon valley.

OPPOSITE, CENTRE The barbecue area (**D**), with substantial stone slabs made into a bench (**8**) and a serving shelf (**9**), has an old window frame placed to accentuate the view over the valley beyond.

OPPOSITE, RIGHT A simple iron garden gate (**1**) invites the visitor to descend to a lower terrace. The echoing of the geometric shapes, but set at different angles, of the rotund clipped box tree and the grinding stone placed on the gate pier is typical of the ornamental principles which govern this garden.

THE POWER OF PAINT

LEFT TOP The entrance gate (**1**), flung wide in welcome, sets the scene for an uninhibited use of colour, the gate post blue and the gate yellow.

LEFT CENTRE The path forks beyond the entrance gate left towards a table also painted in blue and yellow (**3**), close to an ivy-clad hut with a yellow door. To the right it veers along this stony informal winding way, relieved by an inset pattern of brick and decorative pineapple finials (**5**).

LEFT BOTTOM Along the pineapple path, a pretty yellow gate (**6**) opens to a path leading to the house.

RIGHT Encircled with bright apple green, the front door is the culmination of a series of yellow approach gates. The eves of the house and a support for climbers pick up the blue first encountered on the post of the entrance gate. Evergreen topiary follows the long-standing American tradition of planting clipped evergreens next to the house.

FAR RIGHT Looking back from the front door to the yellow picket gate (**6**), a decorative arch (**7**) frames a Matisse sculpture (**4**) set on a pedestal painted in the usual blue. The approach planting is an unusual mixture: on one side a floriferous border encroaches on the path, on the other a straight low box hedge encloses a higher zigzag hedge, also of box.

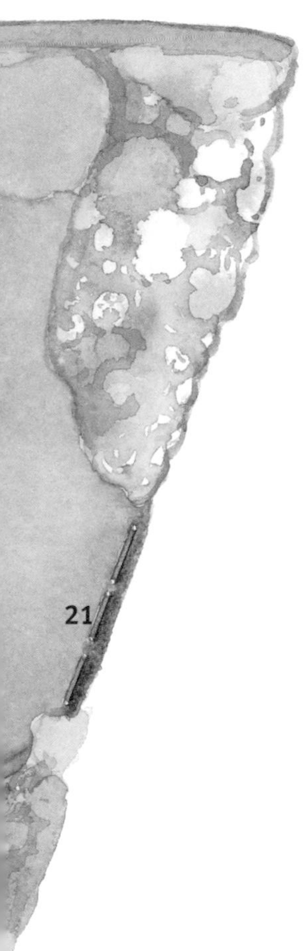

AREAS OF THE GARDEN

A Gravel entrance terrace
B User-friendly maze
C Flower garden
D Potager
E Magnolia thicket

ORNAMENTAL FEATURES

1 Yellow entrance gate
2 Table and chairs
3 Yellow table with jug
4 Matisse sculpture
5 Pineapple path
6 Yellow picket gate
7 Yellow archway and gate
8 Mauve bench
9 Beethoven tribute
10 Willow plant supports
11 Painted fencing
12 Stairway to viewing platform
13 Bench opposite entrance gate to potager
14 Laburnum tunnel
15 Water feature
16 Hermit's hut
17 Wooden walkway
18 Gazebo
19 Gingko and box ball grove
20 Yellow and blue Rietveld seats
21 Mauve fencing

OPPOSITE, LEFT An intriguing tableau has been made for a metal jardinière, arranged with glass cloches and pot plants to form a shrine to Beethoven (**9**). The cast of the head has been gilded and sited at an unexpectedly low level inset into invasive ivy. Touches of gold always add lustre to the garden scene.

OPPOSITE, RIGHT The terrace along one side of the house is of a simple brick pattern with an edging of rectangular concrete slabs. It is held in by wooden balustrading with yellow balusters. A still life has been formed of handsome plant-filled containers alternating with willow pyramids (**10**), which will perhaps be used as supports for climbers later in the growing season.

Like several other gardens in this book, this is an artist's garden, that of the distinguished American painter, Robert Dash. Artists invariably have an originality of vision which enables them to break out of clichés and blaze a path for others to follow. The garden, in the state of New York, is not that large but so crammed with innovative ideas about ornament that only a section of it can be included here. If this garden has a single message to give, it is not to be afraid of using strong colour. Lilac, green, blue, yellow and purple are resolutely used here with all their pristine punch on the house, fences, arches, gazebos, seats and gates, with no attempt to soften their impact through weathering. Indeed, their impact is sustained through regular painting so that they retain their freshness.

What is so striking is that the result does not quarrel with garden features that are not modernist or even post-modernist, but firmly in the revivalist style of the 1980s when the world of Lutyens and Jekyll along with that of the Arts and Crafts movement in England was rediscovered and re-created. We see the innovative side by side with an unashamedly romantic garden: a laburnum tunnel (**14**), a potager peopled with clipped box together with traditional topiary (**D**) and paths which mainly adhere to the principle of using natural materials.

All of this is a refreshing reminder that a garden in an overwhelmingly nostalgic traditional style can be compatible with a bold contemporary statement which shouts that colour in the garden need not only come from flowers. The garden furniture is also far from being the usual period pastiche but very much of the present age: angular, almost aggressive and heavy in form, but enlivened by the same gaiety of colour. And, once the blossom of spring and summer has faded, what could be more cheerful on a dull day in winter than these sunny yellow gates and arches? This kind of colour in the garden gives year-round value.

Nor is the owner afraid of the idiosyncratic in other ways. His love of Beethoven's music finds concrete expression in a gilded head arranged almost on a horticultural altar of celebration (**9**). A flight of wooden steps painted blue (**12**) takes visitors up to the flat roof of the house to look down on the garden in much the same way as in earlier centuries one might have ascended a mount for the view. A grove of gingko trees is unexpectedly

A simple laburnum tunnel (**14**) gives a new twist to the predominantly blue and yellow theme of the painted decoration. When the laburnum is in flower in the spring the tunnel offers a dazzling variant on the all-pervasive combination of blue and yellow with the advent of a shower of brilliant yellow panicles set against the blue-painted structure. This is a classic instance of drawing the eye: the simplest of wooden structures is punctuated halfway along its length by a modest trickling fountain (**15**) framed against an arched trellis screen in the distance.

interspersed with large balls of glossy green clipped box (**19**) and a fence looking into the countryside beyond is painted bright mauve (**21**). There is a hermit's hut embowered in a cascade of roses (**16**), and more of the lilac colour in the gazebo (**18**), which is structured like a park bandstand, cheerfully clashing with the blue and yellow chairs (**20**) based on those designed by the artist Rietveld in the early twentieth-century.

At first glance all this might seem almost arbitrary but in fact both the choice and the disposition of the colour is carefully programmed, moving from the welcoming yellows of the entrance gates, arches and doors and on through to the lilacs of the gazebo and fencing beyond. Where does one place this combination of old and new in stylistic terms? One might describe it as Gertrude Jekyll meets Andy Warhol, for colour of this kind comes directly out of the Pop Art movement of the 1960s with its unapologetic use of blocks of primary colour. This is a healthy reminder that the world of the decorative arts, of which garden ornament is a branch, often follows rather than anticipates contemporary trends in the visual arts. As a consequence the Dash garden has a strange dual resonance. Take away the brightly painted artefacts and we could be in a garden made before 1914. Put them back and we have added the world of Roy Lichtenstein and Robert Indiana along with all those who burst upon the art scene in the early 1960s. Looking at it in this way, it has taken almost a generation for that aesthetic to affect the garden.

The lessons to be drawn are myriad. The garden bids you to choose your palette and link house and garden, something all too rarely done. Use solid colour and avoid the distressed look. If you make a mistake first time round in your choice of colour, alter it by simply repainting. Remember that colour of this kind needs to be set off by an abundance of greens and never, but never, use a colour wheel, something which the art student is told to throw away on arrival at college. This will release you to embark on what would otherwise be regarded as startling and original combinations of a kind nature herself cheerfully indulges in. In a small space there will only be room for a limited number of artefacts using colour in this definite way. My strongest advice would be to concentrate on using it to draw the house into the composition.

RIGHT ABOVE A viewing platform (**12**) is a rare feature in today's gardens but, before the era of the landscape style, was an almost universal feature used for looking down upon the patterns of knots and parterres. This vantage point provides a general panorama of this part of the garden. Contrary to expectation, the pretty picket fence painted lilac (**11**) is in no way discordant amid the jostling explosion of white and magenta flowers.

RIGHT BELOW The potager (**D**) at the back of the house is in fact more parterre than potager, geared for aesthetic effect rather than productivity, because the invasive roots of the box take nutrients from the vegetables. None the less this is a charming example of the revival of the decorative potager which was such a feature of the 1980s. Held in by a sturdy picket fence lined with wire netting to keep out the rabbits, the design is a simple symmetrical geometric pattern of narrow paths of concrete slabs with a forest of sculpted box balls and vertical topiary arranged with military precision.

LEFT A grove of gingko trees arises from greensward punctuated by large clipped box balls providing bold sculptural form at ground level (**19**). Box is drought-tolerant and flourishes beneath the dappled light from the trees' leaves. Beyond, a circle of columnar cypresses surrounds an open-work wooden gazebo (**18**) painted in striking shades of lilac-mauve and pink.

BELOW Inside the gazebo, in addition to the table and chairs, is the somewhat eccentric addition of a Victorian wash basin and jug, which are of a kind also placed on the table (**3**) at the entrance to the garden. The circular 'windows' frame interesting views in every direction. The view here is towards fencing (**21**), painted the same shade as the gazebo, which marks the garden's boundary. Countryside lies beyond it.

SCALE & SIMPLICITY

←

A wall fountain is an ideal addition to almost any tiny town garden. At one stroke it brings movement, sound and reflected light into the most enclosed and confined of spaces, as well as opportunities for a modest display of aquatic and marginal plants. And it can be in almost any style from the classically inspired Italianate *bocca* to the strictly contemporary solution we see in this minute Belgian garden, made by its owners, the architects Claes and Humblet. Minimalist simplicity has been achieved here, with two cantilevered triangles jutting from the base of a pilaster in a brick wall (**1**), the water gently flowing into a shallow, square, concrete-capped container planted with waterlilies. Around it is modest, mainly green, planting. The area has been articulated with decking at three different levels on which plants in containers are arranged in season. Tender plants may overwinter in the greenhouse (**2**) through which the garden is reached from the house. Contrasting curved sculptural form is provided by a large clipped box (**3**). No combination could be simpler or more stylish. The owners have added a still life of stones on the rim of the fountain's bowl (**4**) and utilized the practical but antique metal watering cans to the same effect (**5**).

Much of the success of this garden is owed to the scale of the water feature. In such a confined area, it is the focus of attention, making a confident, major statement. It is also a striking demonstration of how the style of a set piece like this affects everything else in the garden, including the hard landscaping and the planting. If the wall fountain had been a more conventional stone lion's head, for example, it would have demanded a quite different style of garden to set it off to best advantage.

LEFT Seen from the house over a window box of white busy lizzie flowers, a single pleached lime (**6**) at the end of the garden provides an aerial hedge giving privacy. The subtle changes in level in the decking articulate what might otherwise have been a dull flat surface. The main focus of attention remains the watery centrepiece.

RIGHT A lesson in economy of means and sheer inventiveness, the wall fountain (**1**) is a traditional *bocca* in abstract guise.

ORNAMENTAL FEATURES

1 Wall fountain
2 Greenhouse
3 Clipped box mound
4 Still life of stones on concrete ledge
5 Antique watering cans
6 Pleached lime screen

SPATIAL SORCERY

The garden at The Arrow Cottage, in Herefordshire, was designed by its owner Lance Hattatt. Elegant and ambitiously compartmented, it is orchestrated by a complex arrangement of vistas and cross-axes. The style stems from Edwardian gardens such as Hidcote, in Gloucestershire, a series of rooms, each with its own theme, linked by passages formed from hedges of yew and beech. The area seen on these pages is in fact only part of a much larger garden, but even within this restricted space there are several different themes, including a peony walk (**15**), a herb garden (**C**), Mediterranean borders (**E**), and a summer-house garden (**G**). But the most spectacular feature is the rill cascade (**2**) with focal points at either end: a two-storey tower (**3**) and a *jet d'eau* (**1**) in the centre of a gravel circus. It is an object lesson in the manipulation of a small, irregular space through the imaginative use of vista: capturing the eye by means of ornament makes the area seem much larger than the reality.

The irregularity of the site has been completely concealed by introducing the rill as a bold central spine in an area where it could be as long as possible. The other gardens fall pell-mell either side of it. Twin avenues of yew hedges and pots planted with agapanthus draw the eye to the yellow gothic tower at one end and to the fountain at the other. The tower is placed so that it catches the evening sun, making a perfect place for summer dining. The slanting rays of the sun also enhance the warm golden colour that it is painted. Even without the rill this would be a dramatic garden ensemble, but the water adds movement, sound and sparkle.

RIGHT At one end of the rill cascade (**2**), a single jet of water (**1**) arises from a circle of stone and gravel, with a halo of flower pots and a containing bed filled with lime green *Alchemilla mollis*. It is screened by clipped beech.

FAR RIGHT The tower (**3**) acts as a focal point at the other end of the rill. Two young yew hedges, still feathery and awaiting clipping, are already performing their task of drawing the eye to the tower, a progression aided by the pots of agapanthus on either side of the water course. When siting the tower, the owners were astute enough to take full advantage of a mature tree as a backdrop.

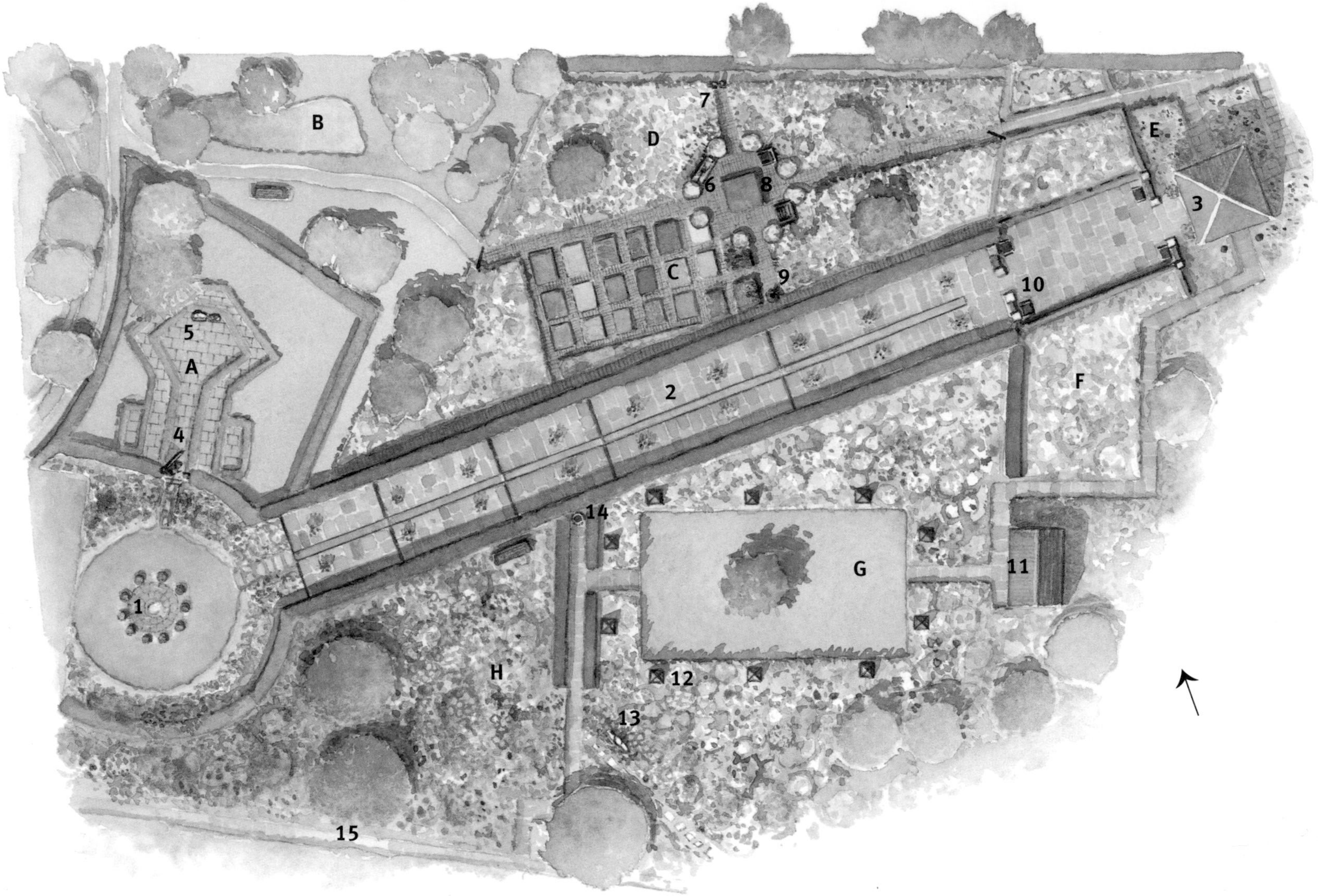

The success of the tableau owes much to the size and hue of the tower. The lesson it teaches is about scale: never be afraid of large features or bright colour in a small space. Another, less costly way of achieving a similar effect would be to erect a large trellis screen with an arch at its centre framing a statue or a large urn, the trellis painted yellow or perhaps bright blue or apple green. A ready-manufactured arbour could serve the same purpose, if given height by the simple expedient of raising it up on a terrace approached by a flight of steps. Even part of the façade of the house could be used, but it would have to be symmetrical with a central door, porch or window which, if not handsome, should be enhanced. A vista as controlled as this calls for an eye-catcher at both ends.

AREAS OF THE GARDEN

A An arena providing space for outdoor events
B The pond garden
C The herb borders within the kitchen garden
D Hot colour borders within the kitchen garden
E The Mediterranean borders planted in cool colours
F Borders planted in white colours
G The summerhouse garden
H The rose garden

ORNAMENTAL FEATURES

1 *Jet d'eau*
2 The water rill
3 Yellow tower
4 Gateway
5 Statues
6 Reclining stone figure
7 Totem figures
8 Pair of seats
9 Terracotta vase
10 Four blue-painted seats
11 Summerhouse containing bench and inscription
12 Blue obelisks
13 Crouching figure statue
14 Classic stone vase on plinth
15 Peony walk

LEFT The summerhouse (**11**) looks down the rectangular garden named after it from the centre of one end, providing both a viewpoint and a focal point. A commodious garden seat in the summerhouse has been painted a gorgeous rich carnation pink. Beautifully incised above is a quote from Virgil: 'It is always spring or summer here.' Inscriptions always add meaning to a building. The idiom is a Renaissance one asking the visitor to pause and think through its connotations and what it says about the particular place.

RIGHT The summerhouse garden (**G**) consists of a rectangular lawn surrounded by herbaceous borders, which are punctuated by deep blue wooden obelisks (**12**) that support and add architectural contrast to the lush planting. (One of the yew hedges defining the rill cascade can be seen in the background.)

RIGHT What was once the kitchen garden is now dominated by three generous borders planted for late summer colour. It is divided into four quarters, one of which contains the herb beds (**C**) arranged like a paintbox. The garden uses a raised platform of clipped box at its centre, at the crossing of the two major axes, making a calm, green focal point among the mass of brilliant yellows and oranges. This is the garden behind one of the hedges along the rill cascade (**2**). The viewpoint gives a tantalizing glimpse of the tower (**3**) in the distance, emphasizing the excitement of having a major ornament that can be seen from almost anywhere in the garden.

LEFT TOP A pair of wooden totem figures by Terry Ryall (**7**) terminate a short vista along one of the cross-axes of the kitchen garden.

LEFT MIDDLE Ornament as incident: a recumbent stone figure (**6**) whose belly collects rainwater, by Helen Sinclair, nestles in one of the corners at the centre of the hot colour borders (**D**). A wooden armchair (**8**), one of a pair, has been placed in the opposite corner to look towards it.

LEFT BOTTOM · A simple terracotta vase (**9**), set on the ground, with a trophy of dried globe artichokes from the nearby herb beds (**C**), makes an effective focal point at the end of the cross-axis opposite the totem figures (**7**). Behind it rises one of the yew hedges that flank the rill cascade (**2**).

EXOTIC REFLECTIONS

This is a garden of unashamed theatricality that taps into a centuries-old tradition of garden ornament as stage scenery. Its two creators, Earl Hyde and Susan Bennett, are both artists unafraid of striking out in new directions, and, over a period of some twenty-five years, they have transformed what could have been a conventional small urban back garden of a modern house in London into a visual extravaganza. Its centrepiece is a dazzling blue rotunda (**3**) of the owners' invention, but other brilliantly coloured ceramic artefacts of their own making, as well as discarded objects like a fibreglass fake Louis XV fireplace surround (**1**) are used to give an overall impression of exoticism. The impact is heightened by the use of mirror glass in doors that lead nowhere (**7**) but double the garden's vista and reflect the ceramic tiles, pagodas, pots and treillage in blues and scarlets and touches of glittering gold. Two ponds (**2** and **4**) with small waterfalls add to the shimmering effect not only with reflections and movement but also because they are filled with goldfish.

The whole fantasy is held together by an abundant use of evergreen plants, making this a garden that is particularly stunning in winter. Covering about a third of an acre, the garden seeks to impose a lively asymmetry on a rectangular site by disguising the perimeters with planting and with the use of curved borders and serpentine lines.

RIGHT The rotunda (**3**) is a triumph of improvisation: the columns are of gas-main piping slipped over fence posts set into concrete; the bases and capitals were modelled in ceramic by the owners; the cornice is of plastic-clad plywood and the cupola, made in two parts and topped by a pine cone, is of fibreglass. The whole construction was painted and gilded by the owners. It is set off in summer by a planting of hostas.

FAR RIGHT One of the simplest of ornament ideas, a door always suggests more beyond it. In this instance that 'more' is met by the use of mirror glass, which reflects the main vista across the garden (**7**). The awning, the red lacquer paint, as well as the use of gravel and planting of dwarf conifers and a purple-leaved acer, heighten the aura of chinoiserie.

FAR LEFT Utilitarian objects of yesteryear become, through time, the collectibles of the present. A Victorian mangle which began its life in a country cottage was retrieved from a dusty shed. Now, enlivened by being painted blue and gold, it makes an unusual incident and talking point (**9**).

LEFT This Louis XV-style fibreglass reproduction fireplace (**1**) was thrown out by neighbours when they redecorated the room in which it stood. Its use as a garden ornament is unexpected and original, made even more so by the lustrous marbling in blue, scarlet and gold. A fender has been added in Victorian edging tiles and filled with a clever planting to suggest a fire in *Coleus blumei*, *Sansevieria trifasciata* and the copper-leafed pelargonium 'Black Night'.

FAR RIGHT AND RIGHT The delightful red and blue ceramic pagoda (**5**), made by the owners, stays out all year. In harsher climates it could be damaged by frost, but moveable ornaments such as this can be taken inside each winter. The ponds are the two features that require high maintenance in this garden. They are never emptied and rely on filters, which need cleaning twice a week during the summer, to ensure an environment suitable for fish. Thanks to the movement provided by the waterfalls, these ponds have not frozen in winter, but freezing would be a risk with ponds in colder areas. The ceramic paddle steamer (**6**) listing among the water plants adds a touch of quiet within one of the ponds.

AREAS OF THE GARDEN
A House terrace
B Studio terrace
C Gravel terrace
D Greenhouse

ORNAMENTAL FEATURES
1 Fireplace
2 Pond with white pagoda
3 Blue rotunda
4 Pond with waterfall
5 Blue and red pagoda
6 Miniature steamboat
7 Mirrored doorway
8 Oriental-style screening wall
9 Mangle

There are various viewing points in the garden: each one looks in a different direction, providing a multiplicity of vistas. None of these guides the eye back to the house, which is architecturally uninteresting. The L-shape of the house lends itself firstly to an intimate, enclosed vista that leads the eye past a small pool decorated with a white ceramic pagoda (**2**) towards the feathery, pendulous branches of a willow, over which the blue and gold of the rotunda (**3**) can be glimpsed. It is only by walking past the tree that the main sweep of the garden to the larger of the ponds (**4**) becomes visible; and one has to walk further still before the gravelled terrace (**C**), mirrored doors (**7**) and oriental-style screening wall (**8**) come into view. The panorama from the main terrace in front of the studio (**B**) is different but again only takes in part of the garden. Neither the fireplace (**1**) nor the mangle (**9**) are placed as focal points; instead they are minor incidents and come as visual surprises while one walks through the garden.

This garden was not an expensive creation. It is the cumulative work of two people over many years. The various set pieces evolved as more land was acquired and the found objects came their way. Everything in it was asssembled or made by the owners utilizing a wide variety of materials from fibreglass to off-the-shelf piping and door fittings. It is a refreshing reminder that technicolour fantasy in the grand manner does not belong only to the grand gardens of the past. It has potential today, even in the smallest of gardens. All it calls for is boldness of vision and the nerve not to care what the neighbours think.

INCIDENT AND INTIMACY

The town garden made and owned by the distinguished garden writer Mirabel Osler is based on the late-nineteenth-century Arts and Crafts movement's commitment to natural materials. With its brick, stone, cobbles and wood, and its abundant planting, the garden is undeniably nostalgic and romantic, yet it is also quirky and forward-looking in its unexpected use of mirror glass and colourful paintwork.

Its fundamental success lies in the good geometry and the series of ground-level patterns – a mixture of grey paving stones, setts, handsome glazed tiles and cobbles – which give each space within the garden – a terrace (**C**), the path and two sitting enclosures (**A** and **B**) – its own identity. In a town house that has the main living room on the first floor, attention to pattern that can be seen from above is of crucial importance. A strong underlying structure and a firm emphasis on formality, making use of clipped evergreens as a counterpoint to the billowing planting, have made an ideal container for the garden's many and varied decorative features. Without this controlling framework, the ornaments might have appeared as disconnected clutter. Although something catches the eye everywhere one looks, the clear divisions within the garden prevent one from being overwhelmed: each incident remains subordinate to the whole.

RIGHT A garden shed (**2**) has been transformed by paint and planting. A *trompe l'oeil* window by Jessie Jones affords a 'view' into the shed's contents, and an owl is wittily perched on its ledge. The engulfing montana clematis and planting below pose a question as to where reality ends and illusion begins.

FAR RIGHT The brilliant deployment of space makes full use of contrasting materials and patterns at ground level and of false perspective – the brick path has been tapered to make it appear longer. The flight of steps at the other end of the path leads to another visual trick: a door (**1**) that cannot be opened for it leads nowhere. Other ornaments include a sturdy arch (**9**) with a cut-out bird perched on its summit , brightly coloured folding seats and beautiful hand-crafted pots and jugs arranged for the sheer pleasure of looking at them.

RIGHT The view to the small dining area (**C**) at the back of the house shows how the leitmotif of grey-blue paint has been carried not just through the garden in the seating and pots, but has also been used to link the garden and the house.

OPPOSITE, BELOW In a second sitting area (**B**) at the back of the house, a painted folding chair has been placed next to an old hand pump (**8**). Notice how the golden ochre of the walls provides a sunny illusion on even the dullest of days as well as a sympathetic background for the foliage of the climbers.

OPPOSITE, ABOVE LEFT A slate shelf (**10**) on the outside wall of the house provides an opportunity for a still-life display of hand-thrown pottery.

OPPOSITE, ABOVE RIGHT A minute wall cascade (**12**), using an old trough, has been built into the wall of the terrace near the house. Nothing could be simpler or more in keeping with this garden's commitment to natural materials and effects.

AREAS OF THE GARDEN

A Main sitting/dining area
B Second sitting area
C Seating area on lower terrace

ORNAMENTAL FEATURES

1 False door
2 Shed with *trompe l'oeil* painting
3 Container as *miroir d'eau*
4 Cat House
5 Dry slate vase
6 Mirror glass reflecting pots
7 Bronze bust on plinth
8 Hand pump
9 Wooden archway
10 and 11 Display shelves
12 Wall cascade

ABOVE The focus of the garden's main alfresco sitting area (**A**) is the furniture that has been brought into harmony by all being painted the same colour. Used as the base for a table, the lacy ironwork of an old sewing machine echoes that of the pretty bench. Raised to a good height, a bronze bust of a child (**7**) gives sculptural focus to the area, which is firmly delineated by paving, clipped box and elegant standards arising out of bushes of lavender at the corners.

LEFT Throughout the garden there is a variety of handsome pots – some planted, some empty, some painted, some plain – arranged in tableaux. Here, an ingenious use of mirror glass (**6**), sited at ground level, subtly doubles the still life of pots and pelargoniums. Large sheets of mirror glass in the garden quickly smear. Small pieces, regularly cleaned, offer greater opportunities for intriguing reflections.

ABOVE Known as the Cat House (**4**), the garden shelter in the style of the Wiener Werkstätte of around 1900 was designed by Richard Craven. Painted a symphony of mauves, greys and ochres, it is one of the unexpected features of this garden. Its placing along the path, so that its façade is not seen from the house, obviates any clash of architectural styles. It houses a comfortable cushioned seat and can be used on cool but sunny days. Its view is over to the little area surrounding the slate vase (**5**). Notice also the introduction of water as a mirror merely by filling a capacious container (**3**).

LEFT The dry slate vase (**5**), the focal point of the asymmetrical garden opposite the Cat House (**4**), was made by Joe Smith without using any form of adhesive. Its importance is emphasized by its being placed on a stone pedestal and set on a circle of cobbles at the crossing of narrow brick paths, while knee-height mirror glass increases the illusion of space around it.

PHANTASMAGORIA

This dreamworld was created by the surrealist designer Ivan Hicks for himself within the formal enclosure of an old, walled kitchen garden in Sussex. The images and ornaments scattered around are designed to be read by the visitor in any of a number of ways. Nothing within it has a single meaning but instead a multiplicity of meanings – indeed, as many as the onlookers wish to read into whatever their eyes alight upon, whether that is a typewriter encrusted with house leeks or a stone ball on a folding garden chair. Responses can range the whole gamut from shock, derision, disbelief or outright laughter to contemplative thoughts about the nature of human life, the world of nature and the purpose of the universe.

In this phanstasmagoria, which veers between Dali and Disney, the visual approach is polycentric, asking visitors to move around things which are disposed so as to engage them in a succession of encounters. Modernist in that it pays scant heed to the classical rules of perspective, the layout, perhaps surprisingly, follows the basic rectangular lines of the existing, enclosing walls and makes a regular, balanced geometric pattern based on a central axis. Although the entire garden is not represented here, its heart – a circular mound (**A**) and its immediate suroundings – gives a good picture of the principles at work.

The overall debt to late-twentieth-century developments in the visual arts cannot be ignored. It might come under a category which emerged in the second half of the last century, variously defined as Land Art, Arte Povera, Impossible Art and so on. In these an artist might, for example, arrange circles of natural stone on the floor of an art gallery, evoking the ritual structures of early man but in a modern engineered building. Such art depends on irrationality, the idea that thought, labour

A panorama of the garden focuses on its central mount (**A**). Bizarre artefacts, including metal spirals, finials and angular wooden constructs, are dotted in a seemingly arbitrary way, creating an imaginary landscape whose utter strangeness is immediately intriguing. Far from jarring with the planting, it actually endows the horticultural contribution with a hallucinatory quality.

and material have been expended on fabricating something which has no significance. But in fact such statements do have significance, often left to the onlooker to deduce. In the case of the stone circles, it might be that the stones, like those at Stonehenge, are as old as the hills and immortal whereas the building itself will vanish. Linking the garden experience with exercising the mind is as old as garden making. Only in the nineteenth century did garden design and intellectual ideas part company. Hicks is one of the few designers who has laboured to put it back.

How can we translate what we see here into the average garden? The point is to learn the lesson of release from ornament as cliché, as an immutable repertory with immutable rules. In a garden of this kind ornaments, if such they are, come and go. The result is a constantly shifting panorama which defies the norms of conventional garden design.

LEFT The view from the central mount (**A**) towards the containing brick walls of the old kitchen garden shows the seemingly random placing of ornaments, and indeed the composition is never static – objects come and go at the inclination of the artist. The pedestal which appeared on the previous page, for example, now has different objects placed upon it (**8**). The planting, with a controlled use of colour, is more conventional than the ornaments. Plant training also plays a significant role, for there is every kind of topiary and pleaching, including clipped box hedges and box spirals and pyramids.

AREAS OF THE GARDEN

A Circular-mown mound
B Gravel path
C Perennial planting enclosed by dwarf box hedges
D Gravel path surrounded by marjoram beds

ORNAMENTAL FEATURES

1 Garden tools sculpture
2 Metal disks path
3 Gingko wigwam and box balls
4 Benches
5 Metal sculpture surrounded by golden yews
6 Metal spiral
7 Metal saw 'face' sculpture
8 Stone pedestal with metal spring
9 Chair with stone ball
10 Finials
11 Box spiral
12 Metal spiral in pot
13 Metal spiral
14 Blue cloud-painted furniture installation and typewriter
15 Terracotta and metal wheel figure

LEFT An extraordinary path has been constructed from industrial metal circular plates, found pieces, laid on to gravel (**2**). Gingko trees have been ruthlessly trained to form a wigwam arcade (**3**). A self-seeded giant thistle threatens along a walk further delineated by clipped topiary.

OPPOSITE, CLOCKWISE FROM TOP LEFT Six incidents in this fantastical garden demonstrate that in today's garden almost anything goes in terms of ornament. But closer examination reveals genuine wit and inventiveness as well as thought. The aim is always to provoke, to use ornament deliberately to raise the eternal question mark. A disparate assemblage of wheels and blades, pieces of rusted discarded machinery and terracotta flowerpots mockingly conjure up a figure (**15**). We smile but should we? Garden implements are lifted heavenwards in a seeming celebration of the gardener's art (**1**). The blade of a rotary saw stares out at us questioningly (**7**). Is this friend or foe? A topsy-turvy tableau of old chests of drawers with the drawers open, some filled with grasses and flowers, has a filigree ironwork Victorian table seemingly floating above it (**14**). Is this merely junk or is it about the horrors of urban burglary? Sempervivum plants sprawl across an old typewriter placed on a sewing machine base, while the distended fingers of a shop window figure dangle above (**14**). What are our reactions meant to be? A swirl of rusted metal echoes the contorted tree next to it (**13**). Is this nature into art? or art into nature?

A PERSONAL PASSION DISPLAYED

LEFT Against a predominantly green backdrop, a fabricated bird's nest is placed on a folding seat (**16**) in a flower border, multi-coloured bird boxes festoon a tree (**15**) and a slatted bench is decorated with a still life in summer (**14**).

RIGHT All moveable and all connected with birds, in wood, stone, ceramic or metal, these six incidents are scattered through the garden. They can be domestic, as the duck on a trough (**12**), the hen sprouting lavender sitting on a seat (**13**) or the bird perched on a hefty tripod (**3**). They can also be zany, like the scrap of wood to which a metal head and claws has been attached, making a bird that looks as if it is laughing (**1**). The pair of cut-out metal painted birds (**10**) can be picked up as you pass by and made to perch elsewhere. An old ladder painted blue provides support for a bird box and wire baskets filled with knotty twigs (**11**), and a round surface is a perch for more ducks (**9**).

The owner and maker of this small garden, Marlies Tubes, is passionate about birds. Reflecting the ecological preoccupations of an age in which bird populations have plummeted through pollution and the use of pesticides and herbicides, she has turned her suburban garden in north-wewt Germany into a bird sanctuary of two kinds – for both real and ornamental creatures. The layout and the planting of the garden are of the simplest: a rectangle of well-kept green turf is surrounded by borders filled largely with evergreen shrubs to give plenty of shelter and cover for local birds. Against a backcloth of shaggy conifers planted round the boundaries are set holly, choisya, hydrangeas, ivy and ferns. Boldly articulated foliage is counterpointed by mounds of clipped box, a few small flowering trees add height to the composition, and occasional blooms – the tall spires of foxgloves or the frothy heads of hydrangea flowers – fleck the green framework. The demand for maintenance is minimal.

On to this canvas has been embroidered an essay in moveable ornament – virtually everything here can be moved at will. The presence and preoccupations of the owner are woven into the picture by means of a shifting kaleidoscope of ornamental birds of all kinds, from stone ducks, ceramic hens and carved wooden songbirds to stylized birds in painted metal silhouettes. What further unites them is the fact that most can be picked up at any time and rearranged as the whim takes the owner, providing incident wherever she thinks fit. Sometimes they are made to perch on walls or tables, sometimes they nestle on the ground. The surprise and delight of this approach to ornament is that it has both a sincerity and a tongue-in-cheek quality which brings a smile to the face of the beholder. Even a flowerpot sits in a cachepot like a twiggy bird's nest.

This is an ample demonstration that even with the most modest of means – and here the ornaments are all inexpensive craft or mass-produced pieces – a garden can be given a very distinctive identity that reflects the owner's personal interests. All it calls for is conviction and a firm decision not to be seduced by the cliché-ridden repertory of the average garden centre.

1
2
3
4
5
6
7
8
9
10
11
12
13
14
15
16
17
18

ORNAMENTAL FEATURES

1 Tablescape with laughing bird on trough
2 Tablescape with pots of box cuttings
3 Wooden bird on tripod stool
4 Brick seat with flower pots
5 Blue chair with ceramic hens
6 Moveable table and chairs for alfresco dining
7 Brick frame for barbecue with cut-out birds
8 Ceramic ducks and hens
9 Blue table with collection of ceramic ducks
10 Pair of painted cut-out metal birds
11 Blue-painted ladder, bird box andwire baskets
12 Stone duck on trough
13 Stone hen on blue chair
14 Tablescape on slatted bench, and stone balls on turf
15 Dead tree supporting painted bird boxes
16 Red chair with bird's nest
17 Terracotta pots on chimney pots
18 Display shelf

RIGHT Dead trees do not necessarily call for immediate felling. Often they can be made into ornaments by being used as plant supports, painted or, as here, turned into a haven of apartments for the local bird population (**15**). Painting these simple nesting boxes a variety of hues adds year-round colour to the garden as well as bestowing a toy-town quality on it.

VIVA FORMALITY

ABOVE A topiary tableau frames the front door to the house, with box corkscrews (**1**) in pots at either side of the entrance tucked within beds held in by decorative wattle edging (**2**). These are filled with a spring planting of tulips including dark magenta 'Queen of Night'. All the topiary could be purchased fully trained.

RIGHT A view over the maze (**B**) shows a glimpse of the front garden (**A**) to the left. The raised walkway (**E**) leading to an upper floor of the house forms an ideal viewing platform for the maze, the orchard (**C**) and the parterre (**D**) at the back of the house.

The dividing line between topiary and ornament is a fine one, the difference being simply that one uses living plants, albeit trained and clipped, whereas the other is static and complete from the outset. Designed by Thierry Juge, this garden of an old priory in France, makes the point vividly with its lavish use of clipped shiny-leaved dwarf box to give structural form and vertical interest to an area which would otherwise be a dull stretch of grass. The space has been divided into four compartments: a modest arrangement of topiary forming a front garden (**A**) through which a stream runs; a ground-level maze (**B**) of flagstones set into turf with topiary pieces dotted through it; a geometrical orchard (**C**) with more box balls giving it permanent structure; and a gravelled parterre (**D**) at the back of the house which is seasonally planted. The whole is almost entirely enclosed by a most unusual wall made of neatly stacked logs of wood (**4**).

This is a garden whose emphasis on ground-level pattern was prompted by the approach from an upper-floor door and down a flight of steps. All the main gardens can be viewed from the substantial landing at the top (**E**). The composition, stemming from the style of the great French seventeenth-century designer Andre Le Nôtre, demonstrates the difference between French and English formal traditions. In France, different geometric compartments exist side by side whereas in England the urge to introduce dividing hedges would have been almost irresistible, reflecting a passion for privacy and the spell cast by gardens like Hidcote and Sissinghurst. With the addition of hedges the garden's overtly mathematical emphasis would be replaced by mystery and surprise, a journey from reason to emotion.

This could be an almost instantaneous, if expensive, garden for virtually everything except the parterre could be planted for immediate effect. Ground-level mazes, which bring pattern and interest to a plain area of turf, are fun to devise and are a quick way to personalize your garden. To realize how interchangeable topiary and hard-surface ornament can be, it is useful to imagine what the maze would look like if the topiary were replaced by obelisks and statues and the box cushions in the orchard by stone balls.

RIGHT ABOVE The maze (**B**), seen here in winter, retains its interest throughout the year. Four matching three-tiered topiary pieces adorn its central enclosure and the four diagonals that stretch to its corners are emphasized by box pyramids. The log wall (**4**) makes an unusual backdrop.

RIGHT BELOW A symmetrical planting of box provides sculptural ornament in the orchard (**C**), while the box-edged beds of the parterre (**D**) in the foreground are softened with springtime planting. Wooden seats terminate the cross-axes, and a tented pavilion (**9**), used for alfresco meals, is sited at the end of the walk from the upper descent into the garden.

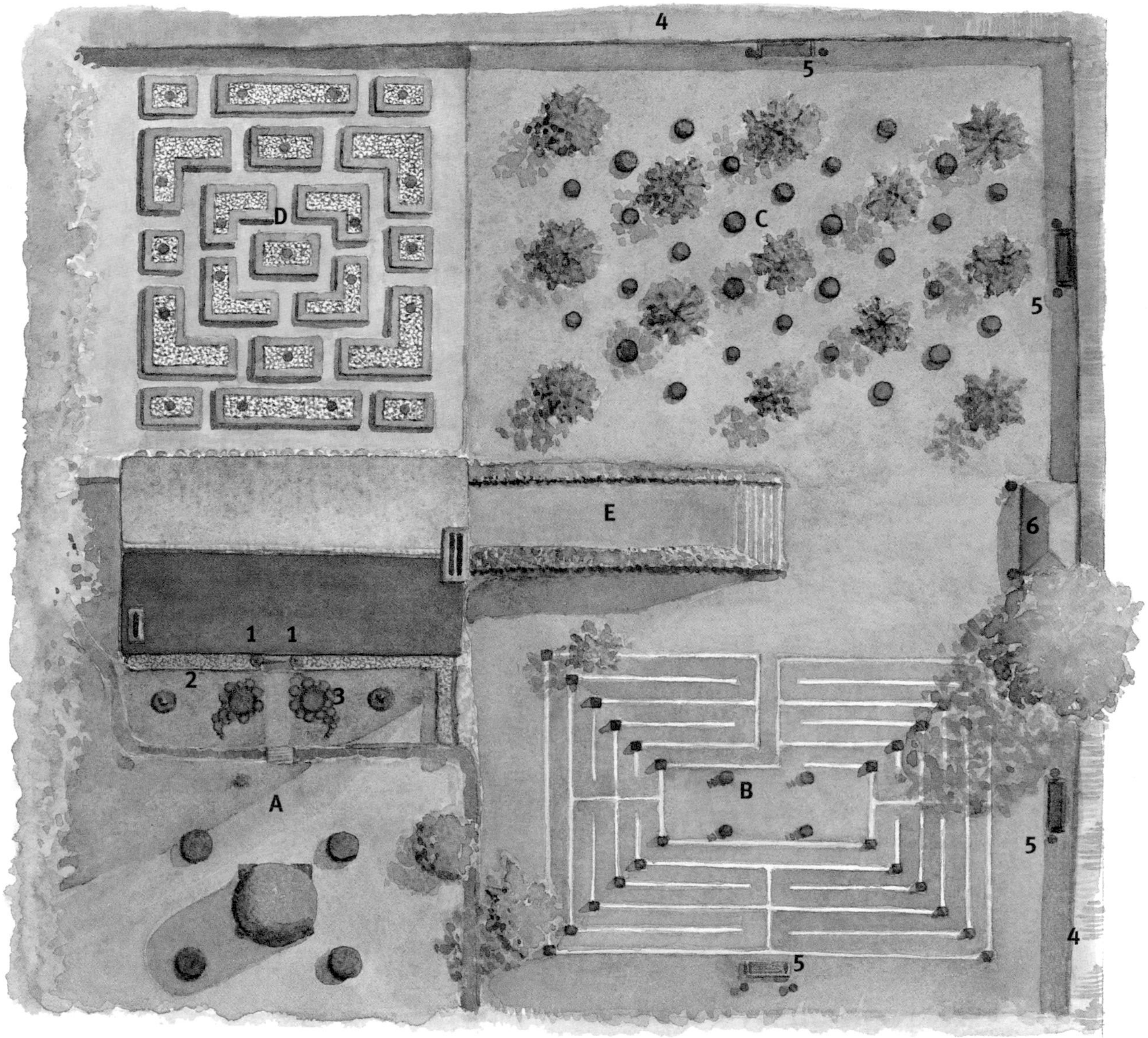

AREAS OF THE GARDEN

A Front garden, with stream running through it
B Maze
C Orchard
D Gravel and box parterre
E Raised platform

ORNAMENTAL FEATURES

1 Box corkscrews
2 Wattle-edged bed
3 Abstract box topiary
4 Enclosing log wall
5 Seats
6 Tented pavilion

INVENTIVE RECYCLING

LEFT AND ABOVE An L-shaped pergola (**5**), made entirely from recycled materials, dominates the garden, providing welcome shade in the summer and year-round drama with its gleaming twisted steel pillars. This is garden ornament used as a statement against the prodigality of our age. The overhead crossbeams are formed from commercial radio antennae and half-inch steel electrical conduits, while the seemingly purely decorative effect of the piers comes from galvanized-steel waterpipes. The abundance of the climbers, the wisteria and grapevines, as well as the underplanting of roses, penstemons and other perennials, are testament to the wisdom of growing only drought-tolerant plants in this dry area of California.

This is a garden which imaginatively responds to the ecological preoccupations of the twenty-first century. Virtually every ornamental effect has come from some demolition site or junkyard. It is the creation of the painter and sculptor John Holmes and his wife Kathleen. Both are passionate about ecology and committed to the notion that we should recycle the waste of our industrial society by putting it to new uses. The garden is set in the Sonoma Valley in California – a fact that needs to be borne in mind when applying any of the exciting ideas here to other, less temperate climates.

A rambling garden of incident, it drifts away from the house into the valley around it through a series of rooms or enclosures, including an orchard (**E**), a vegetable garden (**C**) and a rose-framed gravel exedra (**F**). The whole is held in chiefly by a high wire fence smothered with climbing roses and the fast-growing silver-lace vine, *Polygonum aubertii*, which produces a froth of small white flowers, and partly by a wall of boulders (**A**), which was bulldozed into position and then softened by a planting of lavender and rosemary.

It is a spontaneous garden, for you cannot plan a garden dependent upon recycled materials. Instead the chance to cart away this or that from a demolition site or a salvage yard suddenly presents itself. That is the moment when gardeners must have the vision to see what can be made from what has been jettisoned. Inventiveness is the name of the game – hence the pergola. Other features include an oversize discarded window frame (**6**) that supports a froth of climbing roses, while plastic milk-carton crates have been wired together to form topiary armatures (**4**), and a delightful arbour (**7**) has been created from an old skylight frame by giving it simple timber supports. More eccentrically, the fantasy spirit of the film *The Wizard of Oz* is evoked in the upside-down potting shed (**8**) in the vegetable garden. It was constructed from salvaged windows, but yet it is perfectly practical for its purpose. In this extraordinary creation the owners have not only been true to their ecological principles but also to another tenet they hold dear, the need to surprise. This is also clear in the greensward beyond the confines of the main garden,

FAR LEFT The view across the gravel-pathed vegetable garden (**C**) towards the valley beyond gives glimpses of the pergola and upside-down house (**8**), and shows the high perimeter wire fence not as yet covered with the rampant vine.

CENTRE LEFT The upside-down house (**8**) is both a story-book fantasy and a garden practicality. Constructed by the owner from several discarded windows, the 'front door', complete with wooden steps, is in reality a window, and the door for access is in the 'roof'. It compels attention, drawing on ancient traditions for the garden as a place for wonders.

NEAR LEFT Once inside the upside-down house one discovers that, apart from the dramatic tilt, it is a practical working space with enough light to nurture seedlings and enough space to store essential tools.

AREAS OF THE GARDEN

- A Boulder wall
- B Herb bed
- C Vegetable garden
- D Perennial beds
- E Orchard
- F Rose-framed gravel exedra

ORNAMENTAL FEATURES

1. Bronze pole sculpture
2. Aircraft wing
3. Entrance arch
4. Milk-crate topiary
5. Pergola on twisted steel culverts
6. Rose arbour on window frame
7. Skylight arbour
8. Upside-down house
9. Bronze statue

where part of a shimmering steel aircraft wing (**2**) has been buried in the grass forming an abstract sculpture, and further out still, making a screen for a wooden seat, is a sculpture of bronze disks on metal rods (**1**), which is a private tribute to dead friend.

This is a garden of enormous originality. It asks us to look with fresh eyes at what has been thrown away, and to see its potential for new uses. The opportunities it opens up in terms of garden ornament are boundless for those with the courage to go in that direction. And, startling though all this may seem, it should not be forgotten that the Holmes have used recycled materials to construct items that have been part of the repertory of garden ornament over the ages: the pergola, the arbour, frames on which plants can climb, and a potting and tool shed. These ornamental features are truly the vocabulary of the past in the visual language of today.

ABOVE AND RIGHT Beyond the wall of boulders, which holds the garden in and, with a topping of wire fence, keeps the animals out, there is a patch of lawn into which has been buried the tip of a polished metal aircraft wing (**2**). It has been deliberately placed so that it reflects the rising sun on one side and the setting sun on the other. More found objects, metal plates atop rods (**1**), are arranged to act as sentinels to lead the eye towards the wing from the shade of an ancient oak tree.

THEATRICAL ILLUSIONS

The owner and creator of this garden, Jenny Jones, is a theatre designer, so her preoccupation with manipulating perceptions of space is hardly surprising. Theatre design is about placing people in space, even if that space is illusory, and about controlling how the stage is viewed by the audience. Both are abundantly evident in this highly innovative garden.

The garden stretches to only three-quarters of an acre, but it packs a lot in. It evolved in two phases, which are reflected in gardens on two separate levels, each based on quite different principles. The area immediately outside the old stone-built farmhouse was the starting point. Divided into four distinct compartments, the wide terrace includes a square, wisteria-clad trellis enclosure (**A**), a generous stone and brick path bordered with rich planting, an area of clipped box forming waves (**B**), and a contemplative space where a small pond (**C**) is enlivened by a wind harp (**5**), with two benches near by on which to sit and listen to it (**4**) and from where to see through it (**6**).

This garden leads to, and forms the preface to, the pond house garden on another terrace at a higher level. This new area is firmly enclosed within high walls, which act as physical and visual boundaries when one is inside them, and is divided by high transparent screens. The strictly limited, and therefore highly controlled, views are central to the concept of the garden, all of which can only be seen when one is seated inside the pavilion (**8**). The pavilion, or pond house, which is used mainly for dining, is sunk, so that it is surrounded – except for the entrance walkway – with a rectangular water basin (**D**), decked

A panorama from the first floor of the house looks over the lower terrace, to the pond house garden on a higher level. The terrace includes a black-painted trellis enclosure to the left (**A**), a broad brick and flagstone path, a swathe of young box plants destined to be sculpted into undulating waves (**B**), and, unseen to the right, a small pond. The box is dissected by a narrow walkway (**2–3**) which also runs straight through the pond house gardens, leaving the pavilion with its containing pond to the left and the gravel garden to the right.

AREAS OF THE GARDEN

A Wisteria enclosure
B Box 'waves'
C Small pond
D Water basin
E Gravel garden

ORNAMENTAL FEATURES

1 Black-painted trellis
2 Central boardwalk
3 Door frame with views through to steps leading beyond the garden
4 Oak seat
5 Water harp
6 Bench
7 Gilded metal screen
8 Pond house
9 Black stainless steel wall
10 Black glass walls
11 Polished aluminium ball and circle on ground
12 Glass prism

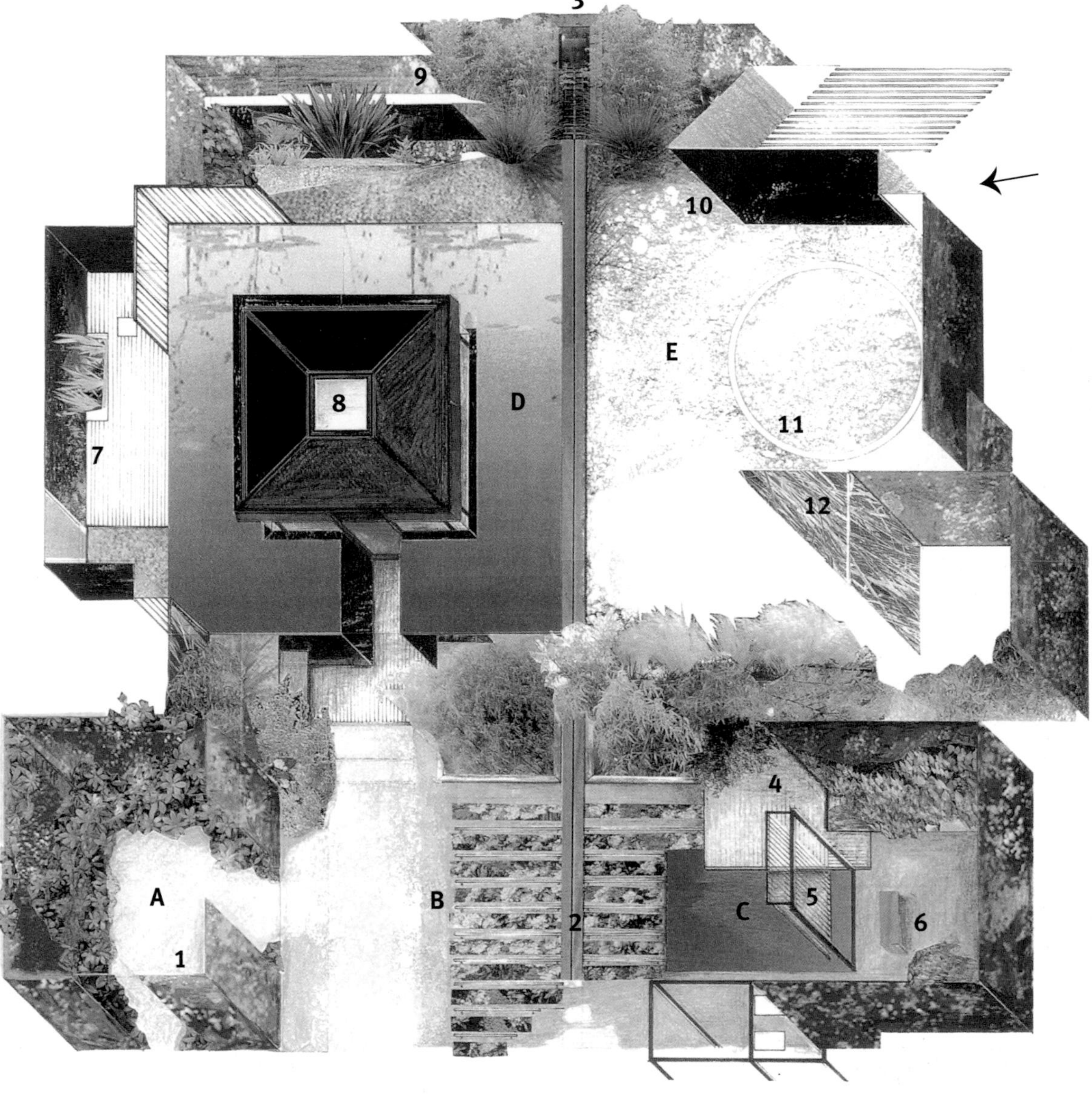

FAR LEFT, TOP One of the views from within the pond house (**8**) looks across waterlilies to a bold planting of spiky phormiums and feathery grasses set against a black stainless-steel screen (**9**) which, according to the time and weather conditions, can be brightly reflective or dark with cast shadow. Window hangings control what the eye can see.

FAR LEFT, CENTRE A decking walk leads to the pond house (**8**), past the containing, waist-high walls of the water tanks (**D**).

FAR LEFT, BOTTOM The gravel garden (**E**), seen through a planting of waving grasses, is held in by walls of black glass (**10**) which define the composition, screen out a lane and protect the plants. The slender silvery trunks of the birches and their fluttering leaves add movement and contrast to the carefully raked gravel.

NEAR LEFT Another view from the pond house looks towards the set piece of a metal screen chequered in distressed gilding (**7**) which responds to light in the grand manner, glinting in the sun's rays. The screen has a horizontal aperture that gives a glimpse of the perennial planting beyond. Once again the scene is framed by the canopy of window blinds.

with colourful marginal plants and waterlilies, that appears to be waist high. Onlookers are deliberately cast at this sub-aqueous level so that they enjoy the magic of the reflections and the panorama of tableaux from an unusual vantage point.

The scenes from the pavilion are both sophisticated and abstract. On one side the view is to an explosion of the sword-like leaves of phormiums set against a wall of black stainless steel (**9**). On another the eye passes over a fringe of waving grasses to a tableau which owes a debt to the gardens of Japan. Here, silver birches flutter against another curtain of black glass (**10**); the gravel at ground level is raked into a 'mountain' to one side while, on the other, a polished aluminium circle (**11**) has been inscribed surrounding a metallic ball. To the right of that, a black bamboo is enfolded by a transparent glass prism (**12**), a feature that elegantly combines the function of a plant

ABOVE LEFT A long narrow boardwalk (**2–3**), emphasized by the line of stainless steel that runs its entire length, bisects the garden. Seen from the lower terrace, it runs up towards a simple door frame in the garden boundary, dividing the pond to the left from the gravel garden on the right.

ABOVE RIGHT The bench (**4**) behind the small pond (**C**) on the lower terrace looks back towards the house. Behind it is the gravel garden (**F**).

ABOVE LEFT A wind harp (**5**) is strung across the small pond (**C**), making a screen behind which a simple bench (**6**) terminates the vista across the lower terrace.

ABOVE RIGHT The bench looks across the full width of the lower terrace, over the box (**B**) and towards the trellis enclosure (**A**). The harp's strings are plucked by the wind, while water trickles down them. The weights at the end of the wires just clear the surface of the water.

protector with the ability to give the viewer almost hallucinatory experiences as the light changes both during the day and through the seasons. On yet another side of the pavilion there are metal panels sporting a chequerboard of distressed metal (**7**) whose shimmering response to sunlight is captured in the inky waters below.

This is a personal and extremely unusual garden. Here the garden building is used less to draw the eye and more to control what it sees. The scenes, like a succession of stage sets, though interconnected, remain self-contained. In a way this is a reinterpretation of the principles of the early landscape garden deployed in a small space. The latter were visited along a set route so that the onlooker was subjected to a series of carefully contrived pictures, although in this instance the visitor is denied entry to them.

LEFT The prism (**12**) in the gravel garden encloses and protects a black bamboo (*Phyllostachys nigra*). Constructed of large three sheets of glass, the prism is another demonstration of the exploration of the effects of hard surfaces in garden making: these are sometimes transparent and at other moments reflective and opaque.

BELOW Seen from the viewpoint of the prism, the gravel garden (**E**) is an elegant minimalist essay with its black glass screens and its ball and circle of polished aluminium (**11**).

INDEX

This view of the garden seen on page 73 reveals the imaginative pebble rectangle acting like a carpet that defines an open-air room in which the furniture is painted a striking shade of blue.

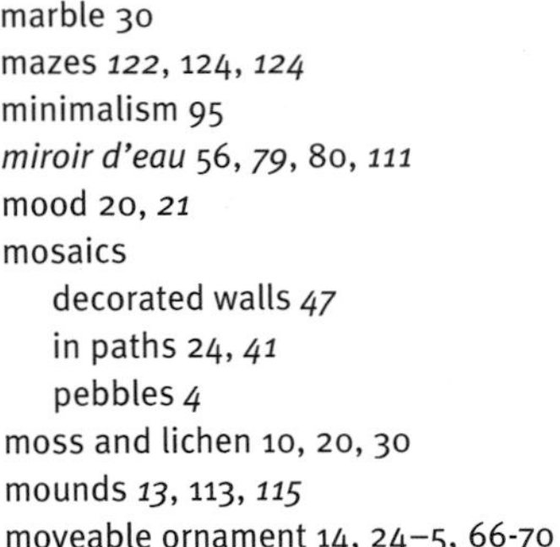

LEFT AND RIGHT A metallic dog romping across the grass and a predatory cat peering at the birds perched on the branches of a tree. Both make you smile. Both can be moved and re-sited at whim.

AUTHOR'S ACKNOWLEDGMENTS

Frances Lincoln had always wanted me to write for her. The saddest fact about this book, my first for her *ab initio*, is that she never lived to see it. She followed it keenly in its initial stages, always sharing my enthusiam for breaking new ground and marrying old and new. It is, therefore, appropriate that I dedicate this to her memory with a real sense of both loss and gratitude.

Such books do not come together without the generosity of those who allow their gardens to be included. I offer them my gratitude. By allowing this intrusion into their private world they will, I hope, inspire other garden-makers to follow in their footsteps.

Nor could such a book exist without the skill and vision of garden photographers. To them I add the team at Frances Lincoln together with the designer, Anne Wilson, and the illustrator, Joanna Logan, who is responsible for the decorative groundplans. They all deserve my heartfelt thanks. R.S.

PUBLISHER'S ACKNOWLEDGMENTS

Artwork by Joanna Logan
Picture research Sue Gladstone
Picture assistant Milena Michalski
Production Kim Oliver
Index Marie Lorrimer

PHOTOGRAPHIC ACKNOWLEDGMENTS

a=above b=below c=centre l=left r=right
d.=designer sc.=sculptor
Clive Boursnell 10 (Sir Roy Strong & Julia Trevelyan Oman, The Laskett, Herefordshire)
Nicola Browne 33 (Arends Nursery); 45 (Steve Martino)
Jonathan Buckley 58r (d. Susan Sharkey)
Jean-Pierre Gabriel 2–3 (Jacques Wirtz); 55 (Mourmans Garden, Belgium); 60l (Scholteshof Garden, Stevoort, Belgium)
Garden Picture Library/Philippe Bonduel 122–123 & 124–125 (d. Thierry Juge, Prieuré Vauboin, France); **Henk Dijkman** 94 & 95 (d. Claes and Humblet, Belgium)
Harpur Garden Library/Jerry Harpur 4–5 (d. Martha Schwartz); 18l (d. Bob Clark, Oakland Hills, California); 21 (d. Mike Springett, Wethersfield, Essex, obelisk/sundial d. David Harber); 23 (d. Dan White, Vancouver); 27 (d. Arabella Lennox-Boyd); 30l (Marcia Donahue, Berkeley, California); 30r & 32 (Phillip Watson, Fredericksburg, Virginia); 36–37 (d. Oehme and van Sweden Associates, Washington, D.C.); 43 (d. Piet Oudolf, Hummelo, The Netherlands); 44 (d. Andrew Pfeiffer, New South Wales); 52br (Charles & Barbara Robinson, Washington, Connecticut); 58l (Chaumont); 60–61 (Hatfield House, Hertfordshire); 72l & 144 (sc. Little & Lewis, Seattle); 74–75 (d. Christopher Masson, London); 86bl & 87r (d. Bob Dash, Sagaponack, Long Island); 116 & 117al (d. Ivan Hicks, Stansted Park, Sussex); 126–127 & 128, 130–131 (d. John & Kathleen Holmes, Penngrove, California); 132–133, 134, 136, 137 & 138–139 (d. Jenny Jones, Garstons, Isle of Wight); **Marcus Harpur** 16–17 (sc. Jonathan Keep, The Garden in an Orchard); 31l (d. Rupert Golby); 54 (Saling Hall, Great Saling, Essex)
Andrew Lawson 7, 11, 12–13 & 15 (Sir Roy Strong & Julia Trevelyan Oman, The Laskett, Herefordshire); 18r (Private Garden, Maine, USA); 25 (sc. Simon Verity, Kiftsgate Court, Gloucestershire); 28–29 (d. Ivan Hicks, Private Garden, Dorset); 34–35 (The Priory, Oxfordshire); 38 (York Gate, Leeds); 39 (Iford Manor, Wiltshire); 40 (d. Susie Lawson); 41l (d. Kate Collity); 46l (d. Andrew Lawson & Tim Neville, Private Garden, Devon); 46–47c (d. Margot Knox , The Mosaic Garden, Melbourne); 50–51 & 66–67c (d. David Hicks); 51r (d. George Carter); 59 (d. Geoffrey Jellicoe, Shute House, Dorset); 63 (d. Piet Oudolf, Hummelo, The Netherlands); 66l (d. John Hubbard, Chilcombe House, Dorset); 70 (d. Sarah Raven, Perch Hill Farm, Sussex); 76–77, 78, 79, 80a & 80b (Gothic House, Oxfordshire); 80c (Gothic House, Oxfordshire, chair d. Paul Anderson); 106–107l (*trompe l'oeil* by Jessie Jones, d. Mirabel Osler, Ludlow, Shropshire); 107r, 108r–109, 110 & 111 (d. Mirabel Osler, Ludlow, Shropshire); 112–113, 117ac, 117ar, 117bl & 117bc (d. Ivan Hicks, Stansted Park, Sussex); 142 (sc. Sophie Thompson)
Marianne Majerus 31r; 53 (Kingston Cottages, Hereford); 56–57 (d. Tessa Hobbs); 62 (d. George Carter); 73 & 140–141 (Emma & Jeff Follas)
Clive Nichols 6 (Sir Roy Strong & Julia Trevelyan Oman, The Laskett, Herefordshire)
Hugh Palmer 20 & 22 (Spring House, Northamptonshire)
Michael Paul 82, 83 & 85 (d. Nicole de Vésian, La Louve, France)
Gary Rogers 1 (d. Alan Sargent, Silver Reflections Garden, Chelsea Flower Show); 8, 9 & 14 (Sir Roy Strong & Julia Trevelyan Oman, The Laskett, Herefordshire); 19l, 52ar, 69l & 143 (Ute & Stephan Kirchner, Germany); 19r (Sigrid Braun); 24 (Graeme & Diane Linfoot, Australia); 26 & 65 (d. Ursula & Klaas Schnitzke-Spijker, Gelnhausen-Hailer, Germany); 47r (d. Dick Dumas); 48–49 (d. Ulrich & Hannalore Timm, Germany); 52l (d. Bunny Guinness, 'A Writer's Garden', Chelsea Flower Show); 67r; 68al (d. Marc de Winter); 68ar, 118, 119 & 121 (Marlies Tubes, Germany); 72r, 86al, 86cl, 86–87l, 88bl, 88br, 90, 91 & 92–93 (d. Bob Dash, Sagaponack, Long Island); 74l (d. Henk Weijers, The Netherlands); 96–97, 98b, 99 & 100–101 (d. Lance Hattatt, Arrow Cottage Garden, Herefordshire)
Elizabeth Whiting & Associates/Nedra Westwater 68b
Steven Wooster 41r (Josie Martin's Garden, Akaroa, New Zealand); 42 & 64 (Les Jardins du Prieuré Notre Dame d'Orsan, France); 58c (d. John Tordoff, Navarino Road, London); 71 (Chaumont); 102–103 & 104 (d. Susan Bennett and Earl Hyde, London); 114 & 117br (d. Ivan Hicks, Stansted Park, Sussex)

Detail of ornament seen on page 72.